To the Student

This book contains 18 high interest stories of recognized literary merit. As the title suggests, each selection in this volume ends with a *sudden twist*. The stories will provide you with hours of reading pleasure—and the exercises which follow offer a variety of ways to help you improve your reading and literature skills.

You will notice that the exercises have been designed to provide a special *twist* of their own:

TELLING ABOUT THE STORY

WATCHING FOR NEW VOCABULARY WORDS

IDENTIFYING STORY ELEMENTS

SELECTING WORDS FROM THE STORY

THINKING ABOUT THE STORY

There are four questions in each of these exercises. Do all the exercises. Then check your answers with your teacher. Use the scoring chart following each exercise to calculate your score for that exercise. Give yourself 5 points for every correct answer.

Since there are four questions, you can receive up to 20 points for each exercise. Use the TWISTS scoring chart at the end of the exercises to figure your total score. A perfect score for the five exercises would equal 100 points. Keep track of how well you do by recording your score on the Progress Chart on page 125. Then write your score on the Progress Graph on page 126 to plot your progress.

TELLING ABOUT THE STORY will help you improve your reading comprehension skills.

WATCHING FOR NEW VOCABULARY WORDS will help you strengthen your vocabulary skills. Often, you will be able to figure out the meaning of an unfamiliar word by using *context clues*—the words and phrases around the word.

IDENTIFYING STORY ELEMENTS will give you practice in recognizing and understanding the key elements of literature.

SELECTING WORDS FROM THE STORY will help you reinforce both your reading *and* your vocabulary skills through the use of the cloze technique.

THINKING ABOUT THE STORY will help you sharpen your critical thinking skills. You will have opportunities to *reason* by drawing conclusions, making inferences, using story clues, and so forth.

An additional section, Thinking More About the Story, offers further opportunities for thoughtful discussion and writing.

On the following page, you will find brief definitions of some important literary terms. If you wish, refer to these definitions when you answer the questions on Identifying Story Elements.

Since there are 18 stories in this collection, you will have the opportunity to read one selection every week of the term, or one selection every other week throughout the school year. Either way, you will enjoy these stories. And the exercises which follow will help you master a number of very important skills.

Now . . . get ready for some *Sudden Twists!*

Burton Goodman

Sudden TWISTS

18 Tales that Take a Surprising Turn

With Exercises for Comprehension & Enrichment

by Burton Goodman

JAMESTOWN PUBLISHERS

a division of NTC/CONTEMPORARY PUBLISHING GROUP
Lincolnwood, Illinois USA

TITLES IN THE SERIES

Sudden Twists

ISBN: 0-89061-501-2

Published by Jamestown Publishers,
a division of NTC/Contemporary Publishing Group, Inc.,
4255 West Touhy Avenue,
Lincolnwood (Chicago), Illinois 60712-1975 U.S.A.

Cover and text design by Deborah Hulsey Christie
Cover illustration by Bob Eggleton

Text illustrations by
Bob Eggleton: pp. 8–9, 28, 40, 58, 65, 76–77, 95;
Pamela R. Levy: pp. 14–15, 46, 71, 89, 108;
Thomas Ewing Malloy: pp. 22–23, 34, 52, 83, 100–101, 115

0 QP 16 15 14

Contents

The Short Story—Literary Terms

Plot: the series of incidents or happenings in a story. The *plot* is the outline or arrangement of events.

Characterization: the ways a writer shows what a character is like. The way a character acts, speaks, thinks and looks *characterizes* that person.

Setting: the time and place of the action in a story; where and when the action takes place.

Mood: the feeling or atmosphere that the writer creates. For example, the *mood* of a story might be joyous or suspenseful.

Theme: the main idea of a story.

Style: the way in which a writer uses language. The choice and arrangement of words and sentences help to create the author's *style*.

Purpose: the reason the author wrote the story. For example, an author's *purpose* might be to amuse or entertain, to convince, or to inform.

1. Cemetery Path

by Leonard Q. Ross

*I*van was a timid little man—so timid that the villagers called him "Pigeon," or mocked him with the title "Ivan the Terrible." Every night Ivan stopped in at the tavern which was on the edge of the village cemetery. Ivan never crossed the cemetery to get to his lonely shack on the other side. The path through the cemetery would save him many minutes, but he had never taken it—not even in the full light of the moon.

Late one winter's night, when bitter wind and snow beat against the tavern, the customers took up their familiar mockery.

Ivan's sickly protest only fed their taunts, and they jeered cruelly when the young Cossack lieutenant flung his horrid challenge at their quarry.

"You are a pigeon, Ivan. You'll walk all around the cemetery in this cold—but you dare not cross the cemetery."

Ivan murmured, "The cemetery is nothing

to cross, Lieutenant. It is nothing but earth, like all the other earth."

The lieutenant cried, "A challenge, then! Cross the cemetery tonight, Ivan, and I'll give you five rubles—five gold rubles!"

Perhaps it was the vodka. Perhaps it was the temptation of the five gold rubles. No one ever knew why Ivan, moistening his lips, said suddenly: "Yes, Lieutenant, I'll cross the cemetery!"

The tavern echoed with their disbelief. The lieutenant winked to the men and unbuckled his saber. "Here, Ivan. When you get to the center of the cemetery, in front of the biggest tomb, stick the saber into the ground. In the morning we shall go there. And if the saber is in the ground—five gold rubles to you!"

Ivan took the saber. The men drank a toast: "To Ivan the Terrible!" They roared with laughter.

The wind howled around Ivan as he closed the door of the tavern behind him. The cold was knife-sharp. He buttoned his long coat and crossed the dirt road. He could hear the lieutenant's voice, louder than the rest, yelling after him, "Five rubles, pigeon! If you live!"

Ivan pushed the cemetery gate open. He walked fast. "Earth, just earth . . . like any other earth." But the darkness was a massive dread. "Five gold rubles . . ." The wind was cruel, and the saber was like ice in his hands. Ivan shivered under the long, thick coat and broke into a limping run.

He recognized the large tomb. He must have sobbed—that was drowned in the wind. And he kneeled, cold and terrified, and drove the saber into the hard ground. With his fist, he beat it down to the hilt. It was done. The cemetery . . . the challenge . . . five gold rubles.

Ivan started to rise from his knees. But he could not move. Something held him. Something gripped him in an unyielding and implacable hold. Ivan tugged and lurched and pulled—gasping in his panic, shaken by a monstrous fear. But something held Ivan. He cried out in terror, then made senseless gurgling noises.

They found Ivan, next morning, on the ground in front of the tomb that was in the center of the cemetery. His face was not that of a frozen man's, but of a man killed by some nameless horror. And the lieutenant's saber was in the ground where Ivan had pounded it—through the dragging folds of his long coat.

TELLING ABOUT THE STORY. Complete each of the following statements by putting an *x* in the box next to the correct answer. Each statement tells something about the story.

1. The young lieutenant challenged Ivan to
   - ☐ a. fight a duel with him.
   - ☐ b. walk to the center of the cemetery.
   - ☐ c. go home alone.

2. Ivan hoped to win
   - ☐ a. five rubles.
   - ☐ b. fifty rubles.
   - ☐ c. twenty pieces of gold.

3. At the end of the story, Ivan could not move because
   - ☐ a. someone was holding him.
   - ☐ b. his legs were frozen stiff.
   - ☐ c. he was pinned to the ground.

4. To win the challenge, Ivan was required to
   - ☐ a. leave a message near the tomb.
   - ☐ b. stick a saber into the ground.
   - ☐ c. report back the next evening.

WATCHING FOR NEW VOCABULARY WORDS. Answer the following vocabulary questions by putting an *x* in the box next to the correct response.

1. The customers jeered Ivan cruelly. What is the meaning of the word *jeered*?
   - ☐ a. questioned
   - ☐ b. cheered
   - ☐ c. made fun of

2. The lieutenant and the villagers made Ivan their quarry. What is the meaning of the word *quarry,* as used in this sentence?
   - ☐ a. a place where stone is cut
   - ☐ b. prey
   - ☐ c. friend

3. With his fist, Ivan beat the sword down to the hilt. Define the word *hilt*.
   - ☐ a. handle
   - ☐ b. tip
   - ☐ c. strength

4. Something gripped Ivan in an unyielding and implacable hold. What is the meaning of the word *implacable*?
   - ☐ a. weak
   - ☐ b. unmoving
   - ☐ c. thoughtful

☐ × 5 = ☐

NUMBER
CORRECT

YOUR
SCORE

☐ × 5 = ☐

NUMBER
CORRECT

YOUR
SCORE

11

IDENTIFYING STORY ELEMENTS. Each of the following questions tests your understanding of story elements. Put an *x* in the box next to each correct answer.

1. What happened first in the *plot* of the story?
   □ a. Ivan pushed the cemetery gate open.
   □ b. The lieutenant gave Ivan a saber.
   □ c. Ivan could not move and cried out in terror.

2. Select the expression which best *characterizes* Ivan.
   □ a. unusually brave
   □ b. very fearful
   □ c. tall and powerful

3. "Cemetery Path" is *set* on
   □ a. an afternoon in fall.
   □ b. a bright summer day.
   □ c. a cold winter night.

4. The *mood* of "Cemetery Path" is
   □ a. humorous and amusing.
   □ b. serious and suspenseful.
   □ c. happy or joyous.

SELECTING WORDS FROM THE STORY. Complete the following paragraph by filling in each blank with one of the words listed below. Each of the words appears in the story. Since there are five words and four blanks, one word in the group will not be used.

Each year, thousands of tourists visit the Père-Lachaise Cemetery in Paris. Some go just to stroll along the beautiful winding _____1_____ . Others feed the _____2_____ , and enjoy a few peaceful moments away from the bustling city. But most go to visit the _____3_____ of the famous people who are buried there. Tourists are a _____4_____ sight at the Père-Lachaise Cemetery in Paris.

tombs   pigeons

familiar

panic   paths

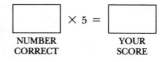

NUMBER CORRECT × 5 = YOUR SCORE

NUMBER CORRECT × 5 = YOUR SCORE

THINKING ABOUT THE STORY. Each of the following questions requires you to think critically about the selection. Put an *x* in the box next to the correct answer.

1. We may infer that Ivan was killed by
   ☐ a. a ghost.
   ☐ b. two villagers.
   ☐ c. terror.

2. Probably, the lieutenant "winked to the men" to show that he was
   ☐ a. afraid of losing the bet.
   ☐ b. confident of winning the bet.
   ☐ c. sorry for Ivan.

3. Clues in the selection suggest that the story takes place in
   ☐ a. Russia.
   ☐ b. England.
   ☐ c. the United States.

4. When the lieutenant discovered how Ivan died, he was probably
   ☐ a. pleased.
   ☐ b. shocked.
   ☐ c. not surprised.

Thinking More About the Story

● The author notes that Ivan wore a long, thick coat. Why is this description important to the story? Suppose that Ivan had not been wearing a long coat. How do you think the story would have ended? Explain your answer.
● Explain why the weather played a very important part in "Cemetery Path."
● Before the conclusion of the story, did you think that Ivan was going to win or lose the bet? Explain your response.

Use the boxes below to total your scores for the exercises.

☐ **T**elling About the Story
\+

☐ **W**atching for New Vocabulary Words
\+

☐ **I**dentifying Story Elements
\+

☐ **S**electing Words from the Story
\+

☐ **T**hinking About the Story
▼

☐ **S**core Total: Story 1

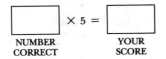

☐ × 5 = ☐

NUMBER   YOUR
CORRECT   SCORE

2. Two Thanksgiving Day Gentlemen

by O. Henry

*I*t was the last Thursday in November—Thanksgiving Day.

As usual, Stuffy Pete took his seat on the third bench to the right as you enter Washington Square Park. Every Thanksgiving Day for nine years he had taken his seat there promptly at one o'clock. And every time he had done so, a wonderful thing had happened to him—something that swelled his heart, as well as his stomach. But today Stuffy Pete's appearance at the usual yearly meeting place was the result of habit, rather than of the hunger he generally felt.

Certainly Pete was not hungry today. He had just come from a feast that had filled him so, he could

15

barely move or breathe. His eyes were like two pale berries firmly buried in a swollen and gravy-smeared mask of putty. His breath came in short wheezes. Buttons that had been sewed upon his clothes a week before by a volunteer from the Salvation Army, flew like popcorn on the earth around him.

Ragged he was, with a split shirt front. But the November breeze, which carried fine snowflakes, brought him only some coolness for which he was grateful. For Stuffy Pete was overheated with the warmth produced by an enormous and magnificent dinner. It had begun with oysters and had ended with plum pudding, and it included, it seemed to him, all the roast turkey and baked potatoes and chicken salad and squash pie and ice cream in the world. Therefore he sat on the park bench and gazed upon the world, full to the brim.

The meal had been an unexpected one. He was passing a red brick mansion near the lower part of Fifth Avenue. In it lived two elderly ladies who believed strongly in tradition. One of their traditional habits was to post a servant outside the house on Thanksgiving Day. They gave him orders to stop the first hungry passerby who came along after the hour of noon and to invite that person in for a banquet. Stuffy Pete happened to be strolling along on his way to the park. Thus it was that he was treated to a feast.

For ten minutes, Stuffy Pete gazed straight ahead. Then he became aware that he desired a slightly different field of vision. With a tremendous effort he moved his head slowly to the left. And then his eyes bulged out with fear. His breath ceased. The ragged edges of his trouser legs brushed nervously up and down on the gravel.

For the Old Gentleman was coming across Fourth Avenue toward his bench.

Every Thanksgiving Day for the past nine years the Old Gentleman had come there and found Stuffy Pete on that bench. Every Thanksgiving Day for nine years he had found Stuffy there, and had led him to a restaurant and watched him eat a huge meal. That was a thing the Old Gentleman was trying to make a tradition of.

The Old Gentleman was thin and tall and seventy. He was dressed all in black, and wore the old-fashioned kind of glasses that won't stay on your nose. His hair was whiter and thinner than it had been last year, and he seemed a bit unsteady and made more use of his big, knobby cane with the crooked handle.

As his benefactor came up, Stuffy shuddered. He longed to flee, but could not bring himself to do so. Moreover, his legs were not capable of the task.

"Good morning," said the Old Gentleman. "I am glad to see that the fortunes of another year have spared you to move in health about the beautiful world. For that blessing alone this day of thanksgiving is well celebrated. If you will come with me, my man, I will provide you with a dinner that should be more than satisfactory in every respect."

That is what the Old Gentleman said every time. Every Thanksgiving Day for nine years. The words themselves were almost an institution. Always before they had been music in Stuffy's ears. But now, with tearful agony, he looked at the Old Gentleman's face. The fine snow almost sizzled when it fell upon the Old Gentleman's perspiring brow. The old fellow shivered a little and turned his back to the wind.

Stuffy had always wondered why the Old Gentleman spoke his speech rather sadly. He did not know that it was because the Old Gentleman was wishing every time that he had a son to succeed him. A son who would stand there after he was gone—a son who would stand proud and strong and would say, "In memory of my father."

But the Old Gentleman had no relatives. He lived quietly by himself on one of the streets east of the park.

Stuffy Pete looked helplessly up at the Old Gentleman for half a minute. The Old Gentleman's eyes were bright with the pleasure of giving. His face was getting more lined each year, but his little black necktie was tied in as neat a bow as ever, and his shirt was beautiful and white, and his gray mustache was curled gracefully at the ends.

And then Stuffy opened his mouth and uttered a noise that sounded like peas bubbling in a pot. Since the Old Gentleman had heard the sounds nine times before, he correctly reasoned that Stuffy had accepted his offer.

"Thank you, sir. I'll go with you, and much obliged. I'm very hungry, sir."

Stuffy's Thanksgiving appetite was not his own. It now belonged to this kindly old gentleman who had taken possession of it.

The Old Gentleman led Stuffy southward to the restaurant, and to the table where the feast had always occurred. There they were recognized.

"Here comes the old guy," said a waiter, "that treats that same bum to a meal every Thanksgiving."

The Old Gentleman sat across the table glowing like a pearl at the sight of Stuffy. The waiters heaped the table with holiday food. And Stuffy, with a sigh that was mistaken for an expression of hunger, raised his knife and fork and began to carve.

No more valiant hero ever fought his way through the ranks of an enemy. Turkey, chops, soup, vegetables, pies, disappeared before him as fast as they could be served. Full to the utmost when he entered the restaurant, the smell of food had almost caused him to lose his honor as a gentleman. But he rallied like a true knight. He saw the look of happiness on the Old Gentleman's face—and he had not the heart to see it grow dim.

An hour later Stuffy leaned back, the battle won.

"Thank you kindly, sir," he puffed like a leaky steam pipe. "Thank you kindly for a hearty meal."

Then he arose heavily with glazed eyes and headed toward the kitchen. A waiter turned him around like a top, and pointed him toward the door. The Old Gentleman carefully paid the bill, and left a tip for the waiter.

They parted as they did each year at the door, the Old Gentleman going south, Stuffy going north.

Around the first corner Stuffy turned. He stood for one minute. Then he seemed to puff out his rags as an owl puffs out his feathers, and fell to the sidewalk like a sunstricken horse.

When the ambulance came, the young

doctor and the driver muttered softly about Stuffy's weight as they placed him inside. Then Stuffy and his two dinners went to the hospital. There they stretched him on a bed and began to test him for various diseases.

And lo! an hour later another ambulance brought the Old Gentleman. And they put him on another bed and mentioned appendicitis, for he seemed to have the symptoms.

But pretty soon one of the young doctors met one of the young nurses he liked, and stopped to chat with her about the cases.

"That nice old gentleman over there, now," he said, "you wouldn't think that was a case of almost starvation. Proud old family, I guess. He told me he hadn't eaten a thing for three days."

TELLING ABOUT THE STORY. Complete each of the following statements by putting an *x* in the box next to the correct answer. Each statement tells something about the story.

1. For the past nine Thanksgiving Days, Stuffy Pete had
   ☐ a. eaten two very large meals.
   ☐ b. enjoyed a feast in a red brick mansion.
   ☐ c. been treated to a meal by the Old Gentleman.

2. The Old Gentleman was sad because he
   ☐ a. had no son to succeed him.
   ☐ b. had lost his fortune through a bad business decision.
   ☐ c. knew that he was very ill.

3. After he left the Old Gentleman, Stuffy Pete
   ☐ a. returned to the bench.
   ☐ b. fell to the sidewalk.
   ☐ c. called a doctor to help him.

4. The Old Gentleman told the doctor that he
   ☐ a. was suffering from appendicitis.
   ☐ b. had just come from a restaurant.
   ☐ c. hadn't eaten for three days.

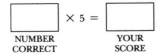

NUMBER CORRECT   × 5 =   YOUR SCORE

WATCHING FOR NEW VOCABULARY WORDS. Answer the following vocabulary questions by putting an *x* in the box next to the correct response.

1. The first hungry person who came by was treated to a banquet. Define the word *banquet*.
   ☐ a. toy
   ☐ b. feast
   ☐ c. fortune

2. For many Thanksgivings, the Old Gentleman had been Stuffy Pete's benefactor. A *benefactor* is a person who
   ☐ a. is always rich.
   ☐ b. gives help.
   ☐ c. is elderly.

3. After a valiant effort, Stuffy Pete finally finished the meal. The word *valiant* means
   ☐ a. brave.
   ☐ b. fearful.
   ☐ c. foolish.

4. For a moment Stuffy thought about fleeing, but his feet were not capable of moving. Which of the following best defines the word *capable?*
   ☐ a. swift
   ☐ b. fortunate
   ☐ c. able

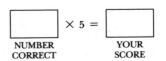

NUMBER CORRECT   × 5 =   YOUR SCORE

19

IDENTIFYING STORY ELEMENTS. Each of the following questions tests your understanding of story elements. Put an *x* in the box next to each correct answer.

1. What happened last in the *plot* of the story?
   □ a. The waiter recognized the Old Gentleman and Stuffy Pete.
   □ b. Stuffy Pete was taken to the hospital.
   □ c. The Old Gentleman was taken to the hospital.

2. Which pair of words best *characterizes* the Old Gentleman?
   □ a. kindly, generous
   □ b. healthy, wealthy
   □ c. lonely, thoughtless

3. The beginning of "Two Thanksgiving Day Gentlemen" is *set* in a
   □ a. mansion on the lower part of Fifth Avenue.
   □ b. park.
   □ c. doctor's office.

4. Which sentence best describes a *theme* of this story?
   □ a. Things are not always what they appear to be.
   □ b. Everyone should be generous during the holiday season.
   □ c. It is foolish to try to help others.

SELECTING WORDS FROM THE STORY. Complete the following paragraph by filling in each blank with one of the words listed below. Each of the words appears in the story. Since there are five words and four blanks, one word in the group will not be used.

Many of the popular dishes that we share with friends and _____ on Thanksgiving Day were introduced to the Pilgrims by Native American cooks. For example, askutasquash, the vegetable we call _____ , was the first food the _____ band of settlers learned to prepare. Other favorites _____ pumpkin pie, cranberries, sweet potatoes and, of course, turkey.

include   **relatives**

bench

squash   **hungry**

	× 5 =	
NUMBER CORRECT		YOUR SCORE

	× 5 =	
NUMBER CORRECT		YOUR SCORE

THINKING ABOUT THE STORY. Each of the following questions requires you to think critically about the selection. Put an *x* in the box next to the correct answer.

1. Although Stuffy Pete was not hungry, he accepted the Old Gentleman's invitation to dinner because Stuffy
   ☐ a. knew that the food would be delicious.
   ☐ b. was glad to have a free meal any time.
   ☐ c. did not wish to disappoint the Old Gentleman.

2. Which of the following is a clue that the Old Gentleman was starving?
   ☐ a. His gray mustache was curled gracefully at the ends.
   ☐ b. He seemed unsteady, and made more use of his cane than ever.
   ☐ c. His eyes were bright with the pleasure of giving.

3. We may infer that the Old Gentleman
   ☐ a. did not really want to treat Stuffy to a meal.
   ☐ b. had been saving money to pay for Stuffy's dinner.
   ☐ c. knew all along that Stuffy had eaten a large meal earlier.

4. Probably, next Thanksgiving Day, Stuffy Pete will
   ☐ a. go to his usual spot in the park.
   ☐ b. decide not to see the Old Gentleman.
   ☐ c. treat the Old Gentleman to a meal.

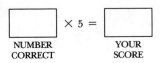

NUMBER CORRECT   × 5 =   YOUR SCORE

Thinking More About the Story

- As usual, the Old Gentleman led Stuffy Pete to a restaurant and watched him eat. The Old Gentleman never ordered anything for himself. On this Thanksgiving Day, what thoughts might have gone through the Old Gentleman's mind as plate after plate of food disappeared before his eyes?
- Should Stuffy, with an explanation, have turned down the Old Gentleman's dinner invitation? Or was he right to accept the feast? Give reasons for your answer.
- Suppose that the Old Gentleman and Stuffy met a little later at the hospital. What do you think each might have said to the other?

Use the boxes below to total your scores for the exercises.

☐ **T**elling About the Story

+

☐ **W**atching for New Vocabulary Words

+

☐ **I**dentifying Story Elements

+

☐ **S**electing Words from the Story

+

☐ **T**hinking About the Story

▼

☐ **S**core Total: Story 2

21

3. The Dinner Party

by Mona Gardner

*T*he country is India. A colonial official
and his wife are giving a large dinner party.
They are seated with their guests—army
officers and government attachés and their
wives, and a visiting American naturalist—
in their spacious dining room, which has
a bare marble floor, open rafters, and wide
glass doors opening onto a veranda.
A spirited discussion springs up
between a young girl who insists
that women have outgrown the
jumping-on-a-chair-at-the-
sight-of-a-mouse era and a
colonel who says that they
haven't.

"A woman's unfailing
reaction in any crisis," the
colonel says, "is to scream. And
while a man may feel like it, he
has that ounce more of nerve
control than a woman has. And
that last ounce is what counts."

The American does not join in the argument but watches the other guests. As he looks, he sees a strange expression come over the face of the hostess. She is staring straight ahead, her muscles contracting slightly. With a slight gesture she summons the servant standing behind her chair and whispers to him. The servant's eyes widen, and he quickly leaves the room.

Of the guests, none except the American notices this or sees the servant place a bowl of milk on the veranda just outside the open doors.

The American comes to with a start. In India, milk in a bowl means only one thing—bait for a snake. He realizes there must be a cobra in the room. He looks up at the rafters—the likeliest place—but they are bare. Three corners of the room are empty, and in the fourth the servants are waiting to serve the next course. There is only one place left—under the table.

His first impulse is to jump back and warn the others, but he knows the commotion would frighten the cobra into striking. He speaks quickly, the tone of his voice so arresting that it sobers everyone.

"I want to know just what control everyone at this table has. I will count three hundred—that's five minutes—and not one of you is to move a muscle. Those who move will forfeit fifty rupees. Ready!"

The twenty people sit like stone images while he counts. He is saying ". . . two hundred and eighty . . ." when, out of the corner of his eye, he sees the cobra emerge and make for the bowl of milk. Screams ring out as he jumps to slam the veranda doors safely shut.

"You were right, Colonel!" the host exclaims. "A man has just shown us an example of perfect control."

"Just a minute," the American says, turning to his hostess. "Mrs. Wynnes, how did you know that cobra was in the room?"

A faint smile lights up the woman's face as she replies: "Because it was crawling across my foot."

TELLING ABOUT THE STORY. Complete each of the following statements by putting an *x* in the box next to the correct answer. Each statement tells something about the story.

1. Mrs. Wynnes knew that a cobra was in the room because she
   - ☐ a. saw it in the rafters.
   - ☐ b. noticed it crawl under the table.
   - ☐ c. felt it on her foot.

2. The American didn't warn the guests about the cobra because he
   - ☐ a. was too frightened to say anything.
   - ☐ b. wasn't sure that there was a cobra in the room.
   - ☐ c. feared that any noise or movement would cause the cobra to strike.

3. The colonel believed that, in a crisis, a woman would
   - ☐ a. always panic.
   - ☐ b. remain very calm.
   - ☐ c. show more control than a man.

4. The cobra came out because it was
   - ☐ a. frightened by the guests.
   - ☐ b. attracted by the milk.
   - ☐ c. awakened by the sound of the American counting.

WATCHING FOR NEW VOCABULARY WORDS. Answer the following vocabulary questions by putting an *x* in the box next to the correct response.

1. The large dinner party took place in a spacious dining room. What is the meaning of the word *spacious?*
   - ☐ a. tiny or small
   - ☐ b. great or vast
   - ☐ c. shabby or run-down

2. The American's first impulse was to jump back and warn the others. Which of the following best defines the word *impulse?*
   - ☐ a. attempt or try
   - ☐ b. information or knowledge
   - ☐ c. instinct or urge

3. Anyone who moved would forfeit fifty rupees. The word *forfeit* means
   - ☐ a. surrender.
   - ☐ b. earn.
   - ☐ c. borrow.

4. At the count of two hundred and eighty, the American saw the cobra emerge. Which phrase best defines the word *emerge?*
   - ☐ a. suddenly strike
   - ☐ b. come into view
   - ☐ c. slip slowly away

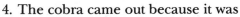

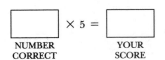

☐ × 5 = ☐

NUMBER CORRECT   YOUR SCORE

☐ × 5 = ☐

NUMBER CORRECT   YOUR SCORE

IDENTIFYING STORY ELEMENTS. Each of the following questions tests your understanding of story elements. Put an *x* in the box next to each correct answer.

1. What happened last in the *plot* of the story?
   - ☐ a. A young girl argued with a colonel.
   - ☐ b. The cobra moved toward the veranda doors.
   - ☐ c. The American began to count to three hundred.

2. Which sentence best *characterizes* Mrs. Wynnes?
   - ☐ a. She was calm and courageous.
   - ☐ b. She became frightened very easily.
   - ☐ c. She was a poor hostess.

3. "The Dinner Party" is *set* in
   - ☐ a. England.
   - ☐ b. India.
   - ☐ c. the United States.

4. Which sentence best expresses the *theme* of the story?
   - ☐ a. Men are more courageous than women.
   - ☐ b. Women are calmer than men.
   - ☐ c. A woman may have as much nerve as a man.

SELECTING WORDS FROM THE STORY. Complete the following paragraph by filling in each blank with one of the words listed below. Each of the words appears in the story. Since there are five words and four blanks, one word in the group will not be used.

Indian snake charmers often

_____ cobras a part of their act.
                    1

These men appear to _____ the
                                        2

snakes by playing a flute. However snakes

are deaf and do not _____ that
                                    3

music is being played. They sway back and

forth because they sense danger. Their

_____ are tense as they hold
            4

themselves on guard, ready to attack.

dinner   **muscles**

know

make   **control**

	× 5 =	
NUMBER CORRECT		YOUR SCORE

	× 5 =	
NUMBER CORRECT		YOUR SCORE

26

THINKING ABOUT THE STORY. Each of the following questions requires you to think critically about the selection. Put an *x* in the box next to the correct answer.

1. In "The Dinner Party," a young girl and a colonel had a difference of opinion. The conclusion of the story suggests that
   ☐ a. the colonel was right.
   ☐ b. the young girl was right.
   ☐ c. both the colonel and the young girl were wrong.

2. Probably, a "strange expression" came over the face of the hostess because she
   ☐ a. saw the cobra in a corner of the room.
   ☐ b. was unhappy that two of her guests were arguing.
   ☐ c. realized that there was a cobra under the table.

3. We may infer that the American decided to count to three hundred because he
   ☐ a. wanted to find out which guests had the most control.
   ☐ b. realized that it might take five minutes for the cobra to come out.
   ☐ c. thought it would make an amusing party game.

4. Which statement is true of both the American and Mrs. Wynnes?
   ☐ a. They were guests at a dinner party.
   ☐ b. They were attacked by a cobra.
   ☐ c. They were quick thinking.

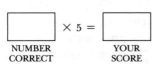

☐ × 5 = ☐

NUMBER   YOUR
CORRECT   SCORE

Thinking More About the Story

● Suppose the American had said nothing at all to the guests. How do you think the story would have ended?
● In the story, a colonel and a young girl have a difference of opinion. With whom do you think the author agrees? Explain your position.
● What do you think the young girl might have said to the colonel after it was revealed that the cobra had been crawling across Mrs. Wynnes' foot? What might the colonel have responded?

Use the boxes below to total your scores for the exercises.

☐
+
Telling About the Story

☐
+
Watching for New Vocabulary Words

☐
+
Identifying Story Elements

☐
+
Selecting Words from the Story

☐
▼
Thinking About the Story

☐
Score Total: Story 3

4. People of the Third Planet
by Dale Crail

$\mathcal{T}$he silver flying saucer hovered silently high above the ground. From far below, on the earth, the craft seemed to be just another star glowing brightly in the dark night sky. Slowly, the spaceship began to descend. It settled in a parking lot near the center of a small sleeping town.

The heat generated by the tremendous craft caused the asphalt on the ground to sizzle. This was the only sound that broke the stillness of the night.

It was about three o'clock in the morning when the alien craft landed. The town was completely deserted. The only sign of activity was a lone traffic light a short distance away. It changed from yellow to red to green over and over again.

For several moments, the ship remained motionless on the ground. Then, slowly, a section of the saucer slid open. Two creatures from another world stepped off the ship and into the light of a street lamp.

For a brief moment, they thought that no one was near. Then they noticed a line of figures standing silently before them.

One of the aliens leaned toward the other and whispered, "Over there are some people of the Third Planet. It is strange that they do not come forward to greet us. Perhaps this is not the time to tell the people of the Third Planet about our world."

The other alien surveyed the figures standing in the dim light. "No," said the alien. "Our charts were right. Our orders are clear. Now is the time. We must approach these Earth people and arrange a meeting with the leader of their world."

The alien stepped forward and began to speak. "People of the Third Planet—or Earth, as you call it. We greet you in peace. We are messengers sent from a world many light years away from your own. We wish to establish a peaceful link between our two worlds and to exchange ideas with you. We would like to speak to someone of importance on your planet. Please direct us to such a person."

No one in the line of figures moved. They remained silent. They did not seem to care about the space creature's words.

After several seconds, a look of bewilderment crossed the face of the alien. "This is strange," whispered the alien to the other. "These earth people act as though they do not understand what I am saying. How can that be? We listened very carefully to their radio signals. We studied their words. I am certain we are using their language correctly."

"Remain calm," said the other alien. "I will speak to the people of the Third Planet again." The alien gazed at the shapes in the darkness then said, "Earth friends, perhaps you were startled by our sudden appearance. Or perhaps you did not fully understand the significance of our message. I can assure you it is of the greatest importance. It is essential that we speak to the leader of your world. Please tell us where we may find your leader."

No one said a word or moved.

"One of you please come forward," continued the alien. "We will not harm you. We wish only to talk with you. However, if you do not cooperate, we will be forced to take one of you with us for questioning. Please, we do not wish to harm anyone."

But the figures in the darkness continued to remain absolutely still.

The alien from another world began to grow angry and glared at them harshly.

"Apparently," said the other alien, "these earth people have no intention of telling us anything. Let us take one of them aboard. We must force one to give us the information we need."

The first alien nodded, then shouted at the figures standing in the dim light. "People of the Third Planet, you have left us no choice! We will have to use force!"

But, to the amazement of the alien, even these words had no effect. The figures did not turn and run. They did not move at all.

Furious, the alien rushed up to the first figure in the line. "You are my prisoner!" shouted the alien. "March to the spaceship at once!"

There was no response.

The alien struck the figure hard. Still, the figure refused to move.

"It is no use," said the alien. "I cannot force this earth person to walk. It is as though he has roots that go deep into the ground."

"Use your ray gun," said the other alien. "Cut him away from the earth he so dearly loves."

There was a single flash from the alien's gun, and the earth person fell noisily to the ground.

Still, none of the other figures moved.

The alien looked at the defiant row of figures before him. They did not seem upset that one of their ranks was being taken prisoner. This was more than the alien could stand.

"People of the Third Planet!" shouted the space creature. "We came in peace, and you refused to speak to us. We took one of your people captive, and you did not attempt to stop us. You are strange people who have no feelings. You baffle me, people of the Third Planet. I will not even try to understand you. I will leave that to another expedition from our plant. Perhaps they will have more success with you than we. Farewell, people of the Third Planet. Farewell!"

The alien turned and joined the other space creature aboard the flying saucer. There was a sudden flash of light, and the spacecraft rose swiftly and disappeared into the night sky.

A patrol car was making its usual rounds on the late night shift. The two police officers inside the car were talking. Suddenly one of them looked up. "What was that?" asked the officer.

"Where? I didn't see anything."

"It looked like an explosion up there in the parking lot. We'd better check to see what happened."

The patrol car sped toward the parking lot and screeched to a halt. The officers jumped out of the car and played their flashlights over the deserted lot.

"Hmmm," said one of the officers. "Something smells burned. Let's look around."

They moved through the area, searching the darkness.

Suddenly, one of the officers called to his partner, "Look at this."

The other officer walked quickly toward the light. He found his partner down on one knee looking at a circular piece of steel which was still hot to the touch.

"Someone sliced off this thing," said the officer. "Did a pretty neat job of it, too. But why? They could only have gotten away with a few nickels. What would anyone want with a parking meter?"

TELLING ABOUT THE STORY. Complete each of the following statements by putting an *x* in the box next to the correct answer. Each statement tells something about the story.

1. The aliens asked the figures in the dark to
   - ☐ a. take them to their leader.
   - ☐ b. tell them about life on their planet.
   - ☐ c. invite them to return again.

2. The figures in the dim light
   - ☐ a. were afraid of the aliens.
   - ☐ b. did not answer the aliens.
   - ☐ c. were happy to see the aliens leave.

3. The aliens thought that the people of the Third Planet were strange because they
   - ☐ a. were awake at three o'clock in the morning.
   - ☐ b. did not seem to have any feelings.
   - ☐ c. could not understand what the aliens were saying.

4. The police officers went to investigate
   - ☐ a. a spaceship which had landed nearby.
   - ☐ b. reports that aliens had landed in town.
   - ☐ c. a suspicious explosion.

WATCHING FOR NEW VOCABULARY WORDS. Answer the following vocabulary questions by putting an *x* in the box next to the correct response.

1. The aliens stated that they brought a message of great significance. What is the meaning of the word *significance?*
   - ☐ a. price
   - ☐ b. size
   - ☐ c. importance

2. "You baffle me," said the alien. "I will not even try to understand you." Define the word *baffle.*
   - ☐ a. puzzle or confuse
   - ☐ b. help or assist
   - ☐ c. recognize or know

3. The heat generated by the tremendous spaceship caused the asphalt to sizzle. The word *generated* means
   - ☐ a. produced.
   - ☐ b. borrowed.
   - ☐ c. cost.

4. The heat generated by the tremendous spaceship caused the asphalt to sizzle. Define the word *sizzle.*
   - ☐ a. fly away
   - ☐ b. make a hissing sound
   - ☐ c. grow cold

	× 5 =	
NUMBER CORRECT		YOUR SCORE

	× 5 =	
NUMBER CORRECT		YOUR SCORE

31

IDENTIFYING STORY ELEMENTS. Each of the following questions tests your understanding of story elements. Put an *x* in the box next to each correct answer.

1. What is the *setting* of "People of the Third Planet"?
   ☐ a. a parking lot
   ☐ b. a spaceship
   ☐ c. a planet many miles from Earth

2. What happened last in the *plot* of the story?
   ☐ a. The alien fired a ray gun.
   ☐ b. The police officer looked at a circular piece of steel.
   ☐ c. The alien ordered a figure to march to the spaceship.

3. Which one of the following statements best *characterizes* the aliens?
   ☐ a. They came in peace to establish a link with another world.
   ☐ b. They were unfriendly and wanted to make war.
   ☐ c. They did not understand the Earth people's language.

4. What is true of the *style* of the story?
   ☐ a. It contains no dialogue.
   ☐ b. There are many long, descriptive passages.
   ☐ c. There are many short sentences.

SELECTING WORDS FROM THE STORY. Complete the following paragraph by filling in each blank with one of the words listed below. Each of the words appears in the story. Since there are five words and four blanks, one word in the group will not be used.

People have always been fascinated by Mars, our neighboring _____ . The surface of Mars appears to be barren and _____ . However, now and then, there are reports of _____ from Mars landing on Earth. So far, though, scientists have not been able to definitely _____ whether or not life exists there. What do you think?

planet   establish

deserted

aliens   town

☐ × 5 = ☐

NUMBER CORRECT   YOUR SCORE

☐ × 5 = ☐

NUMBER CORRECT   YOUR SCORE

THINKING ABOUT THE STORY. Each of the following questions requires you to think critically about the selection. Put an *x* in the box next to the correct answer.

1. The figures in the darkness were
   ☐ a. Earth people who were too frightened to speak.
   ☐ b. some very brave people of the Third Planet.
   ☐ c. a row of parking meters.

2. We may infer that the aliens
   ☐ a. had met people of the Third Planet before.
   ☐ b. knew what the people of the Third Planet looked like.
   ☐ c. had never seen an Earth person before.

3. The police officer thought that a parking meter had been
   ☐ a. destroyed in an explosion.
   ☐ b. stolen by someone.
   ☐ c. sliced off by an alien.

4. When they return home, the aliens will discover that their captive
   ☐ a. still refuses to talk.
   ☐ b. is very frightened.
   ☐ c. will give them the information they desire.

Thinking More About the Story

- Look through the story for hints that the people of the Third Planet were actually parking meters. See how many clues you can discover. Share these with your classmates.
- In what ways did the aliens' civilization seem more advanced than civilization on Earth? Give specific examples. What was surprising about the aliens' behavior?
- Suppose that the two police officers were told that some aliens had just fled with a parking meter. How do you think the police would have reacted?

Use the boxes below to total your scores for the exercises.

☐
+
Telling About the Story

☐
+
Watching for New Vocabulary Words

☐
+
Identifying Story Elements

☐
+
Selecting Words from the Story

☐
▼
Thinking About the Story

☐
Score Total: Story 4

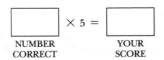

☐ × 5 = ☐

NUMBER CORRECT   YOUR SCORE

5. The Big Day

by Jack Ritchie

There was no question about it, I was now more nervous than I'd ever been before a game. "When do we go out?"

Big Jim Davis looked at his watch. "In ten minutes. Take it easy."

"How's the crowd?"

"Full house. Forty-two thousand people in the stands today."

Forty-two thousand people were in the ball park to watch a big league baseball game. And it wasn't the first day of the season either. It was now September and the pennant races were beginning to tighten up.

But it was the first day in the big leagues for me and I was wondering how I would do out there. This was my big chance. Would I be good enough or would I somehow blow it?

Big Jim sensed how I felt. "You'll do all right, kid. Just keep your mind on the game and don't let anybody rattle you."

Big Jim Davis was a veteran of ten years in the big leagues, never missing a game. A real pro, he was a good man to have on your side. Nothing seems to bother him. He's the kind of a guy who makes it easier for the rest of us and we all respect him.

Forty-two thousand people out there and that was only the frosting on the cake. The game was being nationally televised and that meant that millions of people across the country would also be watching. Staring at the screen. Staring at me.

My throat was dry again, so I walked over to the locker room fountain and took another long drink.

My parents would be before the TV set at home. And my sister too. Actually Mom and Sis never really cared much about baseball—Dad is the real fan—but they would be watching the game today.

I was still young. A rookie. I suppose I'd come up as fast as anybody, but looking back now it seemed like a long, long road stretching into the past.

When I was just a little kid, I would stand on the sidelines watching my father on the playing field and wishing I were out there too. I would follow every ball, every play.

I think Dad could have made it to the top himself. He was that good. But I guess he just never got the breaks. Or maybe other things came first with him, like being with me while I was growing up.

No, Dad hadn't made it to the big leagues, but I knew he was reliving his life in me— following my career and maybe thinking about how it might have been if things had been just a little different.

From the beginning my life was built around the game of baseball, but I could never get really serious about it until after I graduated from high school and was free to do what I wanted with my time. And when you're serious about getting anywhere, you've got to work hard at it full time. You've got to get to know the game forwards and backwards.

There's a lot more to baseball than most people think or see. It isn't all hitting and fielding. There's the mental part, too, and you've got to approach the game with the right attitude.

You've got to learn to take the good days with the bad, knowing that you've always done the best you can and believing that what you're doing is important to the scheme of things.

Even in the off-season, I never let myself get soft or stale. I always kept in shape and watched my diet. I would jog at least three miles every day because I was determined to be in tip-top shape when my big chance came.

Yes, I began right there at the bottom. First the sandlots, then the semi-pros, and then the minors. Places like Des Moines, Appleton, Wisconsin Rapids. And I would spend the lonely nights in small town hotel rooms dreaming about the future I knew would come.

I had been in Wausau when the telegram came. There had been a collision at first base on a close play and when the dust had settled, Robertson lay on the ground with a busted ankle. He was out for the season and they wanted me to report to Baltimore right away.

I had just enough time to pack my suitcases, phone my parents to tell them the news, and then catch a plane to Chicago and from there on to Baltimore.

Now I went to the locker room mirror and stared at myself again.

Yes, I was here. I had finally made it. I had always thought that I was as good as anybody in the game—I had that confidence you needed—but still, right now I was about as tense as a person could be and worried. I took a deep breath. Well, I had come a long way and now it was too late to have any reservations or doubts.

Big Jim looked at his watch again. "Time to earn our money."

I swallowed hard and followed him out the tunnel under the stadium and into the sunlight of the ball park.

After the national anthem was played, I took my position at first base, and the game began.

I was hoping that nothing would come my way—at least not so soon—and it didn't until the third inning.

Evans hit one deep to the shortstop who bobbled the ball for a second before making the throw. It was a close play, but Evans was safe at first.

O'Brien, the first baseman, turned on me with fire in his eyes and the Orioles' manager stormed out of the dugout.

I folded my arms across my chest and put on my best scowl. Let them come. I wouldn't back down an inch. I call them as I see them.

This was my first day and my first play, but I was now a big league umpire.

TELLING ABOUT THE STORY. Complete each of the following statements by putting an *x* in the box next to the correct answer. Each statement tells something about the story.

1. The person who tells this story is
   - ☐ a. a baseball player.
   - ☐ b. the manager of a baseball team.
   - ☐ c. an umpire.

2. Big Jim Davis was
   - ☐ a. a man who had ten years of experience in the big leagues.
   - ☐ b. a first baseman.
   - ☐ c. the owner of a baseball team.

3. The umpire's first play took place
   - ☐ a. right after the playing of the national anthem.
   - ☐ b. in the third inning.
   - ☐ c. at the end of the game.

4. The umpire stated that his Dad
   - ☐ a. never really cared much about baseball.
   - ☐ b. was also a big league umpire.
   - ☐ c. never made it to the big leagues.

WATCHING FOR NEW VOCABULARY WORDS. Answer the following vocabulary questions by putting an *x* in the box next to the correct response.

1. The umpire got his chance because of an injury which occurred as the result of a collision at first base. Define the word *collision*.
   - ☐ a. discussion
   - ☐ b. crash
   - ☐ c. change

2. The new umpire considered himself a rookie. What is the meaning of the word *rookie*?
   - ☐ a. beginner
   - ☐ b. old-timer
   - ☐ c. champion

3. According to a character in the story, baseball is more than hitting and fielding. You must approach the game with the right attitude. Which phrase below best defines the word *attitude*?
   - ☐ a. skills and abilities
   - ☐ b. a way of thinking, acting, or feeling
   - ☐ c. teamwork or cooperation

4. "There's a lot more to baseball than most people think or see," says the narrator. "There's the mental part, too. . . ." What is the meaning of the word *mental*?
   - ☐ a. having to do with the mind
   - ☐ b. having to do with the body
   - ☐ c. having to do with money or wealth

☐ × 5 = ☐

NUMBER CORRECT   YOUR SCORE

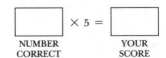

NUMBER CORRECT   YOUR SCORE

37

IDENTIFYING STORY ELEMENTS. Each of the following questions tests your understanding of story elements. Put an *x* in the box next to each correct answer.

1. What happened last in the *plot* of the story?
   ☐ a. The Orioles' manager stormed out of the dugout.
   ☐ b. Robertson broke his ankle.
   ☐ c. The umpire took his position at first base.

2. Which sentence best describes how the main *character* felt?
   ☐ a. He was very relaxed.
   ☐ b. He was confident but nervous.
   ☐ c. He was no longer in tip-top shape.

3. What is the *setting* of "The Big Day"?
   ☐ a. a big league ball park in Baltimore
   ☐ b. a minor league stadium in Des Moines
   ☐ c. a hotel room in Wausau

4. Which sentence best describes the *style* of the story?
   ☐ a. It contains a great deal of dialogue.
   ☐ b. It uses very colorful, poetic language.
   ☐ c. The narrator seems to be having a conversation with the reader.

	× 5 =	
NUMBER CORRECT		YOUR SCORE

SELECTING WORDS FROM THE STORY. Complete the following paragraph by filling in each blank with one of the words listed below. Each of the words appears in the story. Since there are five words and four blanks, one word in the group will not be used.

Jackie Robinson was the first black man to play baseball in the major _____ .
1

In 1947, he was signed by general manager, Branch Rickey, and his great _____
2

as a Brooklyn Dodger began. Jackie's first year was especially _____ because
3

many players and fans were angry that a black player had been hired. That made

Jackie even more _____ to succeed.
4

Just two years later, in 1949, he won the Most Valuable Player award.

tense   career

determined

missing   leagues

	× 5 =	
NUMBER CORRECT		YOUR SCORE

THINKING ABOUT THE STORY. Each of the following questions requires you to think critically about the selection. Put an *x* in the box next to the correct answer.

1. Probably, the umpire was nervous because
   ☐ a. it was his first big league game.
   ☐ b. millions of people were watching.
   ☐ c. both of the above.

2. From what we learn in the story, it seems that
   ☐ a. it is easy to become a big league umpire.
   ☐ b. being a big league umpire is always fun.
   ☐ c. it takes hard work to become a big league umpire.

3. We might expect the Orioles' manager to give this umpire a particularly difficult time because
   ☐ a. he wanted to test him.
   ☐ b. the runner definitely was safe.
   ☐ c. he thought he could get the umpire to change his decision.

4. The next-to-last paragraph of the story suggests that the umpire will
   ☐ a. never make a mistake during his career.
   ☐ b. not be bullied.
   ☐ c. not be respected by the players.

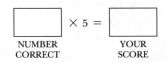

NUMBER
CORRECT
× 5 =
YOUR
SCORE

Thinking More About the Story

● Imagine that several years have passed since the umpire's "big day." What advice do you think the umpire in the story would give a new umpire before *his* first game.

● The speaker says you must "know the game forwards and backwards." Is this more important for a player or an umpire—or must they know the game equally well? Explain your answer.

● Look back through the story for clues which suggest that the speaker is an umpire rather than a player. Make up a *new* clue of your own which hints that the speaker is an umpire.

Use the boxes below to total your scores for the exercises.

Telling About the Story

+

Watching for New Vocabulary Words

+

Identifying Story Elements

+

Selecting Words from the Story

+

Thinking About the Story

▼

Score Total: Story 5

6. The Open Window

by Saki

*M*y aunt will be down in just a few minutes, Mr. Nuttel," said a very calm young lady of fifteen. "Meanwhile, she has asked me to keep you company."

Framton Nuttel tried to think of something appropriate to say. But he was uncomfortable. He *always* felt uncomfortable with strangers. They made him very nervous. In fact, he had come to the country to rest his nerves. And talking to total strangers only served to shake him up more.

"I know how it will be," his sister had said when he was getting ready to leave. "You will stay completely by yourself down there and not speak to a living soul. After a while you'll get so restless, your nerves will be worse than ever. I'll give you the names of the people I knew there—and a letter to introduce you. Some of them, as far as I can remember, were quite nice."

So it was that Framton, with a letter of introduction in his pocket, waited for

Mrs. Sappleton. He wondered whether she was one of the "nice" ones.

"Do you know many of the people around here?" asked the niece, breaking the painful silence.

"No one," said Framton. "My sister was visiting in this part of the country four years ago. She gave me a letter to introduce me to some of the people here." He seemed a little sorry as he said these words.

"Then you know practically nothing about my aunt," the calm young lady went on.

"Only her name and address," admitted the caller. He looked around the room and wondered whether or not Mrs. Sappleton was married. Something about the room seemed to suggest that a man lived there.

"Her great tragedy happened exactly three years ago today," said the girl. "That was after your sister left."

"Her tragedy?" asked Framton. Somehow in this restful country spot tragedies seemed out of place.

"You may be wondering why we keep that window wide open on an October after-noon," said the niece, pointing to a large French window that opened onto a lawn.

"It is quite warm for the time of the year," said Framton. "But has that window got anything to do with the tragedy?"

"Out through that window, three years ago today, her husband and her two brothers went off hunting. They never came back. All three were trapped, and drowned on a treacherous piece of swamp. It had been that very wet summer, you know, and places that had always been safe suddenly became dangerous. Their bodies were never found. That was the terrible part of it."

Here the child's voice began to crack. "Poor aunt. She always thinks that they will come back some day, they and the little brown spaniel that was lost with them. She thinks that they will walk in through that window just as they used to do. That is why that window is kept open every evening until dark. Poor dear aunt, she has often told me how they went out, her husband with his white raincoat over his arm, and Ronnie, her younger brother, singing, 'London Bridge is falling down,' as he always did to tease her, because she said it got on her nerves. Do you know, sometimes on still, quiet evenings like this, I almost get a creepy feeling that they will all walk in through that window—"

She stopped suddenly, with a little shudder. It was a relief to Framton when the aunt finally came into the room. She apologized for being so late.

"I hope Vera has been amusing you," she said.

"She has been very . . . uh . . . interesting," said Framton.

"I hope you don't mind the open win-dow," said Mrs. Sappleton briskly. "My husband and brothers will be coming home soon from hunting. They always enter this way. They've been out in the marsh today, so they'll certainly mess up my poor carpets. So like you menfolk, isn't it?"

She began then to chatter cheerfully about hunting. To Framton, it was horrible. He desperately tried to turn the conversation to a different and less upsetting topic. He was not completely successful, however. At the same time, he realized that Mrs. Sappleton was giving him only a small part of her attention.

Her eyes were constantly looking past him to the open window and to the lawn beyond. It was certainly unlucky that he should have paid his visit just three years to the day when the terrible accident took place.

"The doctors agree that I must have complete rest," announced Framton. He was one of those people who believe that total strangers are hungry for every detail about one's illness. "I must avoid anything that might upset my nerves," he continued. "On the matter of diet they do not agree."

"No?" said Mrs. Sappleton, beginning to yawn. Then she suddenly brightened—but it was not at what Framton was saying.

"Here they are at last!" she cried. "Just in time for tea. And don't they look as if they were muddy up to their eyes!"

Framton shivered slightly and turned towards the niece with a knowing look. But she was staring out through the open window. There was dazed horror in her eyes. In a chill shock of nameless fear Framton swung around in his seat. He looked in the same direction.

In the darkening twilight, three figures were walking across the lawn toward the window. They all carried guns under their arms, and one of them had a white raincoat thrown over his shoulders. A tired brown dog kept close at their heels. As they neared the house, a young voice began to sing: "London Bridge is falling down . . ."

Framton grabbed his hat and ran wildly out of the house. A woman riding along on a bicycle had to run into the hedge to avoid hitting him.

"Here we are, my dear," said the owner of the raincoat, coming in through the window. "It's a bit muddy out, but most of it's dry. Who was that who dashed out as we came up?"

"A most unusual man, a Mr. Nuttel," said Mrs. Sappleton. "He could only talk about his illness, and bolted off without saying a word when you arrived. One would think he had seen a ghost."

"It was probably the spaniel," said the niece calmly. "He told me he had a terrible fear of dogs. He was once chased into a cemetery somewhere on the banks of the Ganges River by a pack of dogs. He had to spend the night in a newly dug grave with the creatures snarling and growling just a few feet above him. Enough to make anyone lose their nerves."

Vera enjoyed making up stories on the spot. She had a talent for doing that.

TELLING ABOUT THE STORY. Complete each of the following statements by putting an *x* in the box next to the correct answer. Each statement tells something about the story.

1. Framton Nuttel went to the country to
   - ☐ a. rest his nerves.
   - ☐ b. go hunting with some friends.
   - ☐ c. have fun at parties.

2. Framton's sister was afraid that he would
   - ☐ a. act foolishly in front of her friends.
   - ☐ b. stop seeing his doctors.
   - ☐ c. spend all his time alone.

3. According to Vera, Mrs. Sappleton's husband and brothers
   - ☐ a. once spent the night in a cemetery.
   - ☐ b. were killed three years ago.
   - ☐ c. were going to return any moment.

4. Vera told her aunt that Mr. Nuttel
   - ☐ a. nearly knocked over a woman riding a bicycle.
   - ☐ b. enjoyed talking about his illness.
   - ☐ c. was terribly afraid of dogs.

WATCHING FOR NEW VOCABULARY WORDS. Answer the following vocabulary questions by putting an *x* in the box next to the correct response.

1. Because he was uncomfortable, it was difficult for Framton to think of something appropriate to say. What is the meaning of the word *appropriate*?
   - ☐ a. proper or correct
   - ☐ b. foolish or silly
   - ☐ c. strange or unusual

2. Places that were safe years ago, had now become treacherous. As used in this sentence, the word *treacherous* means
   - ☐ a. fun.
   - ☐ b. secure.
   - ☐ c. dangerous.

3. Vera told Framton about Mrs. Sappleton's terrible tragedy. Which phrase best defines the word *tragedy*?
   - ☐ a. a realistic dream
   - ☐ b. a very sad event
   - ☐ c. a happy occasion

4. In the distance were three figures, along with a tired brown spaniel. A *spaniel* is a
   - ☐ a. raincoat.
   - ☐ b. dog.
   - ☐ c. rifle.

☐ × 5 = ☐

NUMBER CORRECT   YOUR SCORE

☐ × 5 = ☐

NUMBER CORRECT   YOUR SCORE

IDENTIFYING STORY ELEMENTS. Each of the following questions tests your understanding of story elements. Put an *x* in the box next to each correct answer.

1. The *setting* of "The Open Window" is
   ☐ a. an apartment in the city.
   ☐ b. a room in a country house.
   ☐ c. a swamp somewhere in the country.

2. What happened first in the *plot* of the story?
   ☐ a. Framton grabbed his hat and ran wildly out of the house.
   ☐ b. Vera looked out of the window with horror in her eyes.
   ☐ c. Mrs. Sappleton apologized for being so late.

3. Which statement best *characterizes* Vera?
   ☐ a. She cared deeply about other people's feelings.
   ☐ b. She was extremely honest.
   ☐ c. She was quick witted and creative.

4. Which of the following best describes the author's *purpose* in writing the story?
   ☐ a. to educate or inform
   ☐ b. to amuse or entertain
   ☐ c. to change the reader's mind

SELECTING WORDS FROM THE STORY. Complete the following paragraph by filling in each blank with one of the words listed below. Each of the words appears in the story. Since there are five words and four blanks, one word in the group will not be used.

There are more than ten _____ 1

kinds of dogs in the spaniel family. For

hundreds of years, spaniels have been used

as _____ 2 dogs—especially for

birds. First the spaniel must flush out, or

_____ 3 , the birds into the air. Then,

if the hunter's shot is _____ 4 , the

spaniel finds the bird and brings it to

the hunter.

chase   hunting

remember

different   successful

	× 5 =	
NUMBER CORRECT		YOUR SCORE

	× 5 =	
NUMBER CORRECT		YOUR SCORE

THINKING ABOUT THE STORY. Each of the following questions requires you to think critically about the selection. Put an x in the box next to the correct answer.

1. It is safe to assume that Mrs. Sappleton's husband and brothers
   - ☐ a. almost died in the swamp.
   - ☐ b. were ghosts who had returned.
   - ☐ c. went out hunting earlier that same day.

2. We may infer that Vera knew that
   - ☐ a. the hunters would be returning shortly.
   - ☐ b. Mrs. Sappleton's husband and brothers had been drowned.
   - ☐ c. Framton once spent a night in a newly dug grave.

3. Vera's story had an especially powerful effect on Framton because he
   - ☐ a. didn't believe in ghosts.
   - ☐ b. was so easily upset.
   - ☐ c. was so relaxed.

4. Which of the following facts was probably most important to Vera?
   - ☐ a. It was unusually warm for the time of year.
   - ☐ b. Mr. Sappleton took his raincoat with him when he went hunting.
   - ☐ c. Framton knew practically nothing about her aunt.

☐ × 5 = ☐

NUMBER CORRECT   YOUR SCORE

Thinking More About the Story

- Why was it important for Vera to know that Framton was a stranger to the area? Why did she say that the tragedy took place exactly three years ago?
- When Mrs. Sappleton said, "Here they are at last," Framton turned to the niece with a knowing look. What expression do you think he *expected* to see on her face? What do you think Framton expected to see when he turned to the open window?
- At the end of the story, Vera offered an explanation of why Framton dashed off. Do you think Mrs. Sappleton believed her? Give reasons to support your answer.

Use the boxes below to total your scores for the exercises.

☐
+
Telling About the Story

☐
+
Watching for New Vocabulary Words

☐
+
Identifying Story Elements

☐
+
Selecting Words from the Story

☐
▼
Thinking About the Story

☐
Score Total: Story 6

7. Charles

by Shirley Jackson

The day my son Laurie started kindergarten, he gave up his little-boy clothes and began wearing blue jeans with a belt. I watched him go off that first morning with the older girl next door, looking as though he were going off to a fight.

He came home the same way at lunchtime. "Isn't anybody *here?*" he yelled. At the table, he knocked over his little sister's milk.

"How was school today?" I asked. "Did you learn anything?"

"I didn't learn nothing," he said.

"*Anything,*" I said. "Didn't learn *anything.*"

"But the teacher spanked a boy," Laurie said, "for being fresh."

"What did he do?" I asked. "Who was it?"

Laurie thought. "It was Charles," he said. "The teacher spanked him and made him stand in the corner. He was really fresh."

"What did he do?" I asked. But Laurie slid off his chair, took a cookie, and left.

The next day, Laurie remarked at lunch, "Charles was bad again today." He grinned. "Today Charles hit the teacher," he said.

"Good heavens," I said. "I suppose he got spanked again?"

"He sure did," Laurie said.

"Why did Charles hit the teacher?" I asked.

"Because she tried to make him color with red crayons. Charles wanted to color with green crayons, so he hit the teacher. She spanked him and said nobody play with Charles, but everybody did."

The third day, Charles bounced a see-saw onto the head of a little girl and made her bleed. The teacher made him stay inside during recess.

On Thursday, Charles had to stand in a corner because he was pounding his feet on the floor during story time. Friday, Charles could not use the blackboard because he threw chalk.

On Saturday, I talked to my husband about it. "Do you think kindergarten is too disturbing for Laurie?" I asked him. "This Charles boy sounds like a bad influence."

"It will be all right," my husband said. "There are bound to be people like Charles in the world. He might as well meet them now as later."

On Monday, Laurie came home late. "Charles!" he shouted, as he ran up to the house. "Charles was bad again!"

I let him in and helped him take off his coat. "You know what Charles did?" he demanded. "Charles yelled so much that the teacher came in from first grade. She said our teacher had to keep Charles quiet. And so Charles had to stay after school, and all the children stayed to watch him."

"What did he do?" I asked.

"He just sat there," Laurie said, noticing his father. "Hi, Pop, you old dust mop."

"What does this Charles look like?" my husband asked. "What's his last name?"

"He's bigger than me," Laurie said. "And he doesn't wear a jacket."

I could hardly wait for the first Parent-Teachers meeting. I wanted very much to meet Charles's mother. The meeting was still a week away.

On Tuesday, Laurie said, "Our teacher had a friend come to see her in school today."

My husband and I said together, "Was it Charles's mother?"

"Naaah," Laurie said. "It was a man who came and made us do exercises, like this." He jumped off his chair and touched his toes. Then he sat down again. "Charles didn't even *do* exercises."

"Didn't he want to?" I asked.

"Naaah," Laurie said. "Charles was so fresh to the teacher's friend, they wouldn't *let* him do exercises."

"Fresh again?" I said.

"He kicked the teacher's friend," Laurie said. "The teacher's friend told Charles to touch his toes, and Charles kicked him."

"What do you think they'll do about Charles?" my husband asked.

"I don't know," Laurie said. "Throw him out of school, I guess."

Wednesday and Thursday were routine. Charles yelled during story time and hit a boy in the stomach and made him cry. On Friday, Charles stayed after school again, and so did all the other children.

On Monday of the third week, Laurie came home with another report. "You know

47

what Charles did today?" he demanded. "He told a girl to say a word, and she said it. The teacher washed her mouth out with soap, and Charles laughed."

"What word?" his father asked.

"It's so bad, I'll have to whisper it to you," Laurie said, and whispered into my husband's ear.

"Charles told the little girl to say *that?*" he said, his eyes widening.

"She said it *twice*," Laurie said. "Charles told her to say it *twice*."

"What happened to Charles?" my husband asked.

"Nothing," Laurie said. "He was passing out the crayons."

The next day, Charles said the evil word himself three or four times, and got his mouth washed out with soap each time. He also threw chalk.

My husband came to the door that night as I was leaving for the Parent-Teachers meeting. "Invite her over after the meeting," he said. "I want to get a look at the mother of that kid."

"I hope she's there," I said.

"She'll be there," my husband said. "How could they hold a Parent-Teachers meeting without Charles's mother?"

At the meeting, I looked over the faces of all the other mothers. None of them looked unhappy enough to be the mother of Charles. No one stood up and apologized for the way her son had been acting. No one mentioned Charles.

After the meeting, I found Laurie's teacher. "I've been so anxious to meet you," I said. "I'm Laurie's mother."

"Oh, yes," she said. "We're all so interested in Laurie."

"He certainly likes kindergarten," I said. "He talks about it all the time."

"He's had some trouble getting used to school," she said, "but I think he'll be all right."

"Laurie usually adjusts quickly," I said. "I suppose his trouble might be from Charles's influence."

"Charles?" the teacher said.

"Yes," I said, laughing. "You must have your hands full with Charles."

"Charles?" she said. "We don't have any Charles in the kindergarten in our school."

TELLING ABOUT THE STORY. Complete each of the following statements by putting an *x* in the box next to the correct answer. Each statement tells something about the story.

1. Laurie went off to kindergarten
   □ a. with a smile on his face.
   □ b. wearing little-boy clothes.
   □ c. looking as though he were going to a fight.

2. On the first day of school, the teacher spanked Charles for
   □ a. being late.
   □ b. being fresh.
   □ c. spilling ink.

3. Laurie's mother could hardly wait to go to the first Parent-Teachers meeting because she
   □ a. had never been to the school before.
   □ b. was eager to meet Charles's mother.
   □ c. was eager to discuss all the problems Laurie was having.

4. At the end of the story, Laurie's teacher revealed that
   □ a. Laurie was no trouble at all in school.
   □ b. Charles was a problem in class.
   □ c. there was no one named Charles in the kindergarten.

	× 5 =	
NUMBER CORRECT		YOUR SCORE

WATCHING FOR NEW VOCABULARY WORDS. Answer the following vocabulary questions by putting an *x* in the box next to the correct response.

1. At the Parent-Teachers meeting, no one apologized for the way her son had been acting. What is the meaning of the word *apologized*?
   □ a. acted happily
   □ b. expressed regret
   □ c. arrived late

2. Because Charles injured a little girl, the teacher made him stay inside during recess. As used in this sentence, the word *recess* means a
   □ a. hollow place.
   □ b. quiet spot.
   □ c. time during which work stops.

3. Laurie's mother wondered if Charles was a bad influence on Laurie. A person who is an *influence*
   □ a. has no effect on another person's thoughts or actions.
   □ b. has the power to affect another person.
   □ c. is someone who is very young.

4. Wednesday and Thursday were routine: Charles yelled during story time and hit a boy in the stomach. The word *routine* means
   □ a. very amusing or funny.
   □ b. amazing or hard to believe.
   □ c. usual or regular.

	× 5 =	
NUMBER CORRECT		YOUR SCORE

49

IDENTIFYING STORY ELEMENTS. Each of the following questions tests your understanding of story elements. Put an *x* in the box next to each correct answer.

1. Where is "Charles" *set?*
   ☐ a. at the home of Laurie's teacher
   ☐ b. in a school gymnasium
   ☐ c. at Laurie's home and his school

2. What happened last in the *plot* of the story?
   ☐ a. Charles was so fresh, he was not permitted to do homework.
   ☐ b. Laurie's mother met Laurie's teacher at the Parent-Teachers meeting.
   ☐ c. The teacher washed a girl's mouth out with soap.

3. Which sentence best *characterizes* Charles?
   ☐ a. He is high-spirited and wild.
   ☐ b. He is usually helpful and quiet.
   ☐ c. He is very concerned about the other children's feelings.

4. Which one of the following best describes the *style* of the story?
   ☐ a. It is very suspenseful.
   ☐ b. It has a great deal of dialogue.
   ☐ c. It is very poetic.

SELECTING WORDS FROM THE STORY. Complete the following paragraph by filling in each blank with one of the words listed below. Each of the words appears in the story. Since there are five words and four blanks, one word in the group will not be used.

Children _____ begin kinder-
                 1
garten when they are five years old. It is a

time to get ready for first _____ .
                                      2
In kindergarten, children are taught to draw

with _____ , to use scissors, and
          3
to read the letters of the alphabet. They also

_____ how to get along with other
        4
children. Can you remember when you were

in kindergarten?

learn   teacher

grade

usually   crayons

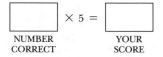

NUMBER CORRECT × 5 = YOUR SCORE

NUMBER CORRECT × 5 = YOUR SCORE

THINKING ABOUT THE STORY. Each of the following questions requires you to think critically about the selection. Put an *x* in the box next to the correct answer.

1. We may infer that Laurie was
   ☐ a. looking forward to starting kindergarten.
   ☐ b. not eager to start kindergarten.
   ☐ c. one of the best students in the class.

2. Laurie's mother thought that Charles's mother
   ☐ a. wouldn't show up at the Parent-Teachers meeting.
   ☐ b. would defend the way Charles had been acting in class.
   ☐ c. would probably be ashamed or embarrassed by Charles's behavior.

3. Evidence in the story indicates that Charles
   ☐ a. often spoke to Laurie at school.
   ☐ b. made friends with all the students in class.
   ☐ c. was Laurie.

4. Probably, Laurie's mother never dreamed that
   ☐ a. there would be so many parents at the Parent-Teachers meeting.
   ☐ b. Laurie's teacher would be so pleasant to her.
   ☐ c. Laurie could be causing problems in school.

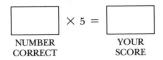

NUMBER CORRECT × 5 = YOUR SCORE

Thinking More About the Story

- Why do you think that Laurie created Charles? Find evidence in the story that Laurie was also a problem at home.
- Although the story is really about Laurie, it is called "Charles." Do you think "Laurie" would have been a better title? How would that have affected the ending? Explain your answers.
- What do you think went through Laurie's mother's mind after she discovered that there was no child named Charles in the kindergarten? What might she have said to her husband after the Parent-Teachers meeting?

Use the boxes below to total your scores for the exercises.

☐ **T**elling About the Story
+
☐ **W**atching for New Vocabulary Words
+
☐ **I**dentifying Story Elements
+
☐ **S**electing Words from the Story
+
☐ **T**hinking About the Story
▼
☐ **S**core Total: Story 7

8. The Getaway

by John Savage

*W*henever I get sleepy at the wheel, I always stop for coffee. This time, I was going along in western Texas and I got sleepy. I saw a sign that said GAS EAT, so I pulled off. It was long after midnight. What I expected was a place like a bunch of others, where coffee tastes like copper and the flies never sleep.

What I found was something else. The tables were painted wood, and they looked as if nobody ever spilled the ketchup. The counter was spick-and-span. Even the smell was OK, I swear it.

Nobody was there, as far as customers. There was just this one old boy—really only about forty, getting gray above the ears—behind the counter. I sat down at the counter and ordered coffee and apple pie. Right away he got me started feeling sad.

I have a habit: I divide people up. Winners and losers. This old boy behind the counter was the kind that they *mean* well. They can't do enough for you, but their eyes have this gentle, faraway look, and they can't win. You know? With their clean shirt and the little bow tie? It makes you feel sad just to look at them. Only take my tip: Don't feel too sad.

He brought the coffee steaming hot, and it tasted like coffee. "Care for cream and sugar?" he asked. I said, "Please," and the cream was fresh and cold and thick. The pie was good, too.

A car pulled up outside. The old boy glanced out to see if they wanted gas, but they didn't. They came right in. The tall one said, "Two coffees. Do you have a road map we could look at?"

"I think so," the old boy said. He got their coffee first, and then started rooting through a pile of papers by the telephone, looking for a map. It was easy to see he was the type nothing's too much trouble for. Tickled to be of service.

I'm the same type myself, if you want to know. I watched the old boy hunting for his map, and I felt like I was looking in a mirror.

After a minute or two, he came up with the map. "This one's a little out of date, but . . ." He put it on the counter, beside their coffee.

The two men spread out the map and leaned over it. They were well dressed, like a couple of feed merchants. The tall one ran his finger along the Rio Grande and shook his head. "I guess there's no place to get across, this side of El Paso."

He said it to his pal, but the old boy behind the counter heard him and lit up like a light bulb. "You trying to find the best way south? I might be able to help you with that."

"How?"

"Just a minute." He spent a lot of time going through the papers by the telephone again. "Thought I might have a newer map," he said. "Anything recent would show the Hackett Bridge. Anyway, I can tell you how to find it."

"Here's a town called Hackett," the tall one said, still looking at the map. "It's on the river, just at the end of a road. Looks like a pretty small place."

"Not any more. It's just about doubled since they built the bridge."

"What happens on the other side?" The short one asked the question, but both of the feed-merchant types were paying close attention.

"Pretty fair road, clear to Chihuahua. It joins up there with the highway out of El Paso and Juarez."

The tall man finished his coffee, folded the map, put it in his pocket, and stood up. "We'll take your map with us," he said.

The old boy seemed startled, like a new kid at school when somebody pokes him in the nose to show him who's boss. However, he just shrugged and said, "Glad to let you have it."

The feed merchants had a little conference on the way out, talking in whispers. Then they stopped in the middle of the floor, turned around, reached inside their jackets, and pulled guns on us. Automatic pistols, I think they were. "You sit where you are and don't move," the tall one said to me. "And *you,* get against the wall."

Both of us did exactly what they wanted. I told you we were a lot alike.

The short man walked over and pushed one of the keys of the cash register. "Every little bit helps," he said, and he scooped the money out of the drawer. The tall man set the telephone on the floor, put his foot on it, and jerked the wires out. Then they ran to their car and got in. The short man leaned out the window and shot out one of my tires. Then they took off fast.

I looked at the old boy behind the counter. He seemed a little pale, but he didn't waste any time. He took a screwdriver out of a drawer and squatted down beside the telephone. I said, "It doesn't always pay to be nice to people."

He laughed and said, "Well, it doesn't usually cost anything," and went on taking the base plate off the telephone. He was a fast worker, actually. His tongue was sticking out of the corner of his mouth. In about five minutes he had a dial tone coming out of the receiver. He dialed a number and told the rangers about the men and their car. "They did?" he said. "Well, well, well. . . . No, not El Paso. They took the Hackett turnoff." After he hung up, he said, "It turns out those guys robbed a supermarket in Wichita Falls."

I shook my head. "They sure had me

fooled. I thought they looked perfectly all right."

The old boy got me another cup of coffee, and opened himself a bottle of pop. "They fooled me, too, at first." He wiped his mouth. "Then I got a load of their shoulder holsters when they leaned on the counter to look at the map. Anyway, they had mean eyes, I thought. Didn't you?"

"Well, I didn't at the time."

We drank without talking for a while, getting our nerves back in shape. A pair of patrol cars went roaring by outside and squealed their tires around the Hackett turnoff.

I got to thinking, and I thought of the saddest thing yet. "You *knew* there was something wrong with those guys, but you still couldn't keep from helping them on their way."

He laughed. "Well, the world's a tough sort of place at best, is how I look at it."

"I can understand showing them the map," I said, "but I'd never have told about the bridge. Now there's not a chance of catching them. If you'd kept your mouth shut, there'd at least be some hope."

"There isn't any—"

"Not a shred," I went on. "Not with a car as fast as they've got."

The way the old boy smiled made me feel better about him and me. "I don't mean there isn't any hope," he said. "I mean there isn't any bridge."

TELLING ABOUT THE STORY. Complete each of the following statements by putting an *x* in the box next to the correct answer. Each statement tells something about the story.

1. The traveler who tells the story stopped to
   ☐ a. buy some gas.
   ☐ b. get some coffee.
   ☐ c. meet an old friend.

2. The two men
   ☐ a. were wealthy feed merchants.
   ☐ b. were heading south on business.
   ☐ c. had robbed a supermarket.

3. The tall man
   ☐ a. shot out a tire.
   ☐ b. ripped out the telephone wires.
   ☐ c. shot the counterman.

4. The town of Hackett is
   ☐ a. surrounded by many other towns.
   ☐ b. not on any highway map.
   ☐ c. at the end of a road on a river.

WATCHING FOR NEW VOCABULARY WORDS. Answer the following vocabulary questions by putting an *x* in the box next to the correct response.

1. According to the counterman, the Hackett Bridge would appear on a recent map. The word *recent* means
   ☐ a. old.
   ☐ b. new.
   ☐ c. folded.

2. A pair of patrol cars went roaring by outside. Which of the following phrases best describes the word *patrol?*
   ☐ a. to protect or observe
   ☐ b. to lose or forget
   ☐ c. to know or understand

3. Both men were paying close attention to the counterman. To pay close *attention* means to
   ☐ a. watch and listen carefully.
   ☐ b. give helpful service.
   ☐ c. stand straight and salute.

4. There was not a shred of hope for the robbers. What is the meaning of the word *shred?*
   ☐ a. a hut or shed
   ☐ b. a jacket or coat
   ☐ c. a very small part

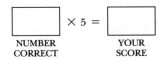

	× 5 =	
NUMBER CORRECT		YOUR SCORE

	× 5 =	
NUMBER CORRECT		YOUR SCORE

IDENTIFYING STORY ELEMENTS. Each of the following questions tests your understanding of story elements. Put an *x* in the box next to each correct answer.

1. Which of the following happened last in the *plot* of the story?
   - ☐ a. The two men looked at the map.
   - ☐ b. The short man shot out one of the tires.
   - ☐ c. The counterman called the rangers.

2. Which of the following best *characterizes* the "old boy" behind the counter?
   - ☐ a. a born loser
   - ☐ b. foolish, easily taken in
   - ☐ c. helpful, sharp-eyed, and clever

3. The *setting* of "The Getaway" is
   - ☐ a. an eating place in Texas.
   - ☐ b. a car somewhere in El Paso.
   - ☐ c. a ranger station near the Rio Grande River.

4. Which of the following statements best expresses the *theme* of the story?
   - ☐ a. One should never eat at an unfamiliar place.
   - ☐ b. You can't always judge what a person is like by a first impression.
   - ☐ c. It isn't wise to be helpful to strangers.

SELECTING WORDS FROM THE STORY. Complete the following paragraph by filling in each blank with one of the words listed below. Each of the words appears in the story. Since there are five words and four blanks, one word in the group will not be used.

The Rio Grande is the sixth longest

_____ in North America. It passes
   ₁

_____ Colorado, New Mexico,
   ₂

and Texas on its journey to the sea. In

Texas, the Pecos River joins it as it makes its

_____ south. From El Paso to the
   ₃

Gulf of Mexico, the Rio Grande is the

boundary line which _____ the
   ₄

United States and Mexico.

> **divides   map**
>
> **river**
>
> **way   through**

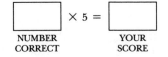

THINKING ABOUT THE STORY. Each of the following questions requires you to think critically about the selection. Put an *x* in the box next to the correct answer.

1. The two men were probably attempting to
   - ☐ a. escape to Mexico.
   - ☐ b. find a bank to rob.
   - ☐ c. visit a friend in Hackett.

2. We may infer that the two men
   - ☐ a. made a successful getaway.
   - ☐ b. drove into the river.
   - ☐ c. returned the money they had stolen.

3. At the end of the story, the narrator probably realized that
   - ☐ a. he had been right all along.
   - ☐ b. the "old boy" was a winner.
   - ☐ c. the robbers were safe in Chihuahua.

4. Which of the following facts plays an important part in the ending of the story?
   - ☐ a. The two robbers were driving a very fast car.
   - ☐ b. One robber was tall and one robber was short.
   - ☐ c. The counterman was about forty and was getting gray.

Thinking More About the Story

- The narrator thinks that the counterman is a "loser." Explain why this is important to the story.
- Why do you think that the two robbers did not suspect that the counterman was leading them astray?
- Suppose the robbers' car got a flat tire after leaving the diner. How do you think the story would have ended? Explain your answer.

Use the boxes below to total your scores for the exercises.

☐
+
Telling About the Story

☐
+
Watching for New Vocabulary Words

☐
+
Identifying Story Elements

☐
+
Selecting Words from the Story

☐
▼
Thinking About the Story

☐
Score Total: Story 8

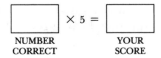

☐ × 5 = ☐

NUMBER   YOUR
CORRECT   SCORE

57

9. The Lion Roared

by Virginia Eiseman

*I*f a Mr. P. Alfred Merivale ever passes your way, you'd better let me know. Just write to me, Mike Brock, assistant manager, at the Mark Twain Hotel, South Plains, Missouri. If you meet P. Alfred, it's a cinch you'll take a long look at him. He's a great big, white-haired guy who wears expensive three-piece suits with silk shirts and ties.

It was a couple of months ago that this P. Alfred Merivale checks in at the Mark Twain Hotel. Minutes after he arrives, Timmy, the bellhop, rushes in, waving a green bill.

"Say, Mike," Timmy yells, "This is one for the books! A big shot from Chicago just pulled in. And guess what he asks for. A *luxury* room! Get a load of that—a *luxury* room!"

Timmy's laughing, and I get a kick out of it, too. The Mark Twain's a fine hotel, but it's not what you'd call a really fancy place.

"This dude must have us mixed up with the Waldorf Astoria," says Timmy. "You ought to see his leather bags—three of the sharpest looking suitcases I've ever had my hands on. And he gave me this ten bucks just for dumping them in his room."

Timmy sticks the bill into his pocket. "Anyhow, Mike," he says, "you'll get a look at this Chicago fellow on account of he's staying two weeks." And then our bellhop breezes out of the lobby.

Well, I don't pay much attention to Timmy's story at first, because he gets emotional when anyone gives him more than a twenty-five cent tip, which isn't very often. But I begin wondering why a stranger would make a point of sticking around South Plains for two weeks. Don't get me wrong. This is a great little town, if you're born and raised here. Still, compared to Chicago, it's a pretty tame place.

At that moment, the lobby door opens and in walks the biggest and most solid-looking citizen I've ever seen. I size him up from top to bottom—from his dark hat to his spanking white shoes. The big guy flashes me a smile.

I say to him in my most hospitable manner, "You must be the gentleman from Chicago. They tell me you're going to be here for quite a spell."

"For two weeks," he nods. "I'm here for a rest. Doctor's orders."

And then I notice something shiny on his suit lapel. I see it's a pin—it's a gold lion pin. At first I think it's one of those pins that colleges hand out, but it's too big for that. I can tell that it's not real gold. And I'm about to ask him just what that gold lion pin

is, when I remember that I'm just the assistant manager, and if the customers go in for silly jewelry—well, that's none of my business.

In the meantime, the man from Chicago's keeping up a steady stream of chatter. Then he plops down on one of the chairs in the lobby, and pretty soon the afternoon gang wanders in and I see that my new pal has joined them.

"I'd like to introduce myself," he's saying. "I'm P. Alfred Merivale from Chicago."

A great session of handshaking and backslapping follows, and in half an hour they're making jokes a mile a minute, and Mr. Merivale's fat pigskin wallet does the honors for sandwiches and cold drinks all around.

Then all of a sudden Cy Archer, our local banker, takes some words right out of my mouth.

"Tell us about that lion pin you're wearing, Merivale," he says.

"Yes," says Ben Woods, "I've never seen anything like it before. Where did it come from?"

"Well, it's a funny thing about this pin," answers Merivale. "I was down in Lima, Peru, about fifteen years ago. One afternoon I wandered into a little shop and bought a lot of trinkets. When I got back to my room and unwrapped the package, this gold pin was on top. I took it back to the man who sold the other articles to me, and he said he'd never seen the pin before. So the only thing for me to do was to keep it."

"Why do you wear it?" Luke Williams asks. "Any special reason?"

The big man turns on his smile full blast.

"That's another funny story. It turned out to be the luckiest little pin anybody ever wore." Mr. Merivale paused for a moment. "Well, gentlemen," he continued, "I realize this is something one doesn't usually discuss, but I've been extremely successful. The reason I mention it is because of the pin. From the second I first saw the lion, the breaks have come my way in everything—oil wells, mines, real estate, the stock market, just everything. And it's all due to this little pin here."

Mr. Merivale laughs. "I wouldn't part with this pin for anything in the world," he says.

Well, during the next week he and his gold lion spend a lot of time in the lobby and the hotel restaurant. You can't believe the number of friends he makes. And it's all on account of the pin.

One morning, Timmy nearly collides with me in the lobby, he's in such a state. "Did you hear the news about Mr. Merivale?" he pants. "He's lost his lion pin."

Right there and then you could have knocked me over with a feather. It seems that the last time Mr. Merivale remembers seeing his pin is at dinner the night before, and now he's offering a thousand dollar reward to anyone who finds it. He's buying a full-page ad in the paper, Timmy tells me.

I feel mighty sorry for Mr. Merivale. He strikes me as being the most high-class customer I've ever met up with. Then I think long and hard about the thousand buck reward, which wouldn't do Mike Brock any harm at all. I can't help wondering if the pin is stolen or lost.

Mr. Merivale shows up the same as usual later in the day. "Maybe I'm carrying this thing too far," he says to the gang. "You fellows must think I'm crazy to promise such a big reward, because the lion's certainly worth no more than a few dollars at most. But that pin means luck to me. I've got to go back to Chicago at the end of the week, and I'm hoping the pin will go with me."

"Don't worry, Alf, we'll find it for you," pipes up Cy Archer.

But we don't find it. Mr. Merivale's loss is the topic of the town all right. People wander about with their eyes glued to the ground, and yet nothing happens.

Finally, the day of P. Alfred's departure rolls around. Right after Timmy brings down his bags, the big man comes over to me.

"I couldn't leave South Plains without telling you goodby, Mike," he says.

I make it clear how sorry I am to see him go, and then we get on the subject of his lion pin.

"That thousand dollar reward still holds," he tells me. "If you ever find a clue, Mike, you can reach me at the Brownstone Hotel in Chicago."

Well, the town seems pretty dreary without Mr. Merivale. Now and then somebody mentions the gold pin, but it still doesn't show up. Everyone acts like there's been a death in the family—they're that fond of P. Alfred. They all keep saying how they wish he'd come back.

One afternoon—it's early and the gang hasn't dropped in yet—I notice a large stranger standing at the end of the lobby. This character hasn't had a shave or a haircut for months. He's wearing a tattered jacket and a pair of pants with patches. One toe is sticking through a hole in his shoe. I say to myself that I'm looking at the original washed-up wreck.

"You'd better move along, Bud," I tell him in a polite way.

Just then my eyes almost pop out of my head. There, sitting on top of a patch in this bum's jacket is Mr. Merivale's gold lion. As fast as I can get the words out, I ask the tramp where he got it.

"Found it by the railroad tracks," is his answer.

I guess I'm making a whole lot of noise 'cause when I finally ask the guy how much he wants for the pin, he thinks for a minute. Then he admits the lion doesn't mean a thing to him. Still, he says, it must mean something to *me* or I wouldn't be making all this fuss, and he says he won't sell it for a cent under five hundred dollars in cash.

I grab my checkbook and pen, and head for the cashier. In a minute I'm back with a wad of bills. They go straight into the bum's grimy fist, and in exchange I get Mr. Merivale's gold pin.

I'm thinking about calling Merivale right away, but I decide that it can wait until after I share my good news with the gang. I'm still congratulating myself, when Cy Archer comes in later with a grin on his face.

"You'll never believe it, Mike," he says. "It's a miracle—an absolute miracle! I just met some broken-down bum outside, and you'll never guess what I bought from him!"

Well, I can guess all right. It's Merivale's gold pin.

A few minutes later, Luke Williams comes in looking mighty happy—and afterwards, Ben Woods, with a big smile on his face. It seems they've each paid some bum $500 for Merivale's lion.

Well, we may not exactly be geniuses, but I can tell you this. If Mr. P. Alfred Merivale is as smart as I know he is, he won't ever again pick South Plains for a rest cure, or come into the Mark Twain Hotel looking for a room.

TELLING ABOUT THE STORY. Complete each of the following statements by putting an *x* in the box next to the correct answer. Each statement tells something about the story.

1. P. Alfred Merivale gave Timmy
   - ☐ a. a gold lion pin.
   - ☐ b. a sandwich and a cold drink.
   - ☐ c. ten dollars.

2. According to Mr. Merivale, the gold lion pin
   - ☐ a. brought him good luck.
   - ☐ b. was given to him by a friend.
   - ☐ c. was stolen by someone at dinner.

3. The bum was willing to give Mike Brock the pin in exchange for
   - ☐ a. a new suit of clothes.
   - ☐ b. a hot meal and a bath.
   - ☐ c. five hundred dollars.

4. Mike Brock is certain that Mr. Merivale
   - ☐ a. could be found at the Brownstone Hotel in Chicago.
   - ☐ b. will never return to South Plains.
   - ☐ c. will visit the Mark Twain Hotel again.

WATCHING FOR NEW VOCABULARY WORDS. Answer the following vocabulary questions by putting an *x* in the box next to the correct response.

1. Timmy got emotional whenever anyone gave him more than a twenty-five cent tip. What is the meaning of the word *emotional?*
   - ☐ a. upset
   - ☐ b. excited
   - ☐ c. very calm

2. The assistant manager spoke to Mr. Merivale in a most hospitable manner. The word *hospitable* means
   - ☐ a. friendly and welcoming.
   - ☐ b. loud and annoying.
   - ☐ c. solemn and serious.

3. According to Mr. Merivale, he found the gold pin in a package of trinkets he had bought. Which phrase best defines the word *trinkets?*
   - ☐ a. ornaments or small pieces of jewelry
   - ☐ b. fancy clothing
   - ☐ c. delicious candies

4. After two weeks, the day of Mr. Merivale's departure finally rolled around. The word *departure* means
   - ☐ a. arrival.
   - ☐ b. leaving.
   - ☐ c. disappointment.

	× 5 =	
NUMBER CORRECT		YOUR SCORE

	× 5 =	
NUMBER CORRECT		YOUR SCORE

IDENTIFYING STORY ELEMENTS. Each of the following questions tests your understanding of story elements. Put an *x* in the box next to each correct answer.

1. The *setting* of "The Lion Roared" is the
   □ a. Brownstone Hotel in Chicago.
   □ b. Mark Twain Hotel in Missouri.
   □ c. Waldorf Astoria Hotel.

2. What happened last in the *plot* of the story?
   □ a. P. Alfred Merivale introduced himself to the afternoon gang.
   □ b. Cy Archer, with a grin on his face, announced a miracle.
   □ c. Mike Brock saw Merivale's lion pin on the jacket of a bum.

3. At the beginning of the story, Mr. Merivale is *characterized* as a
   □ a. wealthy and well-dressed visitor from Chicago.
   □ b. shy man who is under a doctor's orders to rest.
   □ c. foolish fellow who attempts to make himself popular.

4. Which of the following best expresses the *theme* of the story?
   □ a. A stranger tricks some new friends out of money.
   □ b. A lost pin is finally returned to its owner.
   □ c. Some townspeople are saddened when a new friend goes home.

[ ] × 5 = [ ]

NUMBER   YOUR
CORRECT   SCORE

SELECTING WORDS FROM THE STORY. Complete the following paragraph by filling in each blank with one of the words listed below. Each of the words appears in the story. Since there are five words and four blanks, one word in the group will not be used.

When the Dutch _____ in the

New World, they bought Manhattan Island

for twenty-four _____ . That was

truly a bargain. However, if a shady-looking

_____ offers to sell you the

Brooklyn Bridge for a low price, you had

better beware. It might turn out to be the

most _____ mistake you'll ever

make.

compared   **arrived**

stranger

dollars   **expensive**

[ ] × 5 = [ ]

NUMBER   YOUR
CORRECT   SCORE

THINKING ABOUT THE STORY. Each of the following questions requires you to think critically about the selection. Put an *x* in the box next to the correct answer.

1. Which one of the following was probably true of the pin?
   ☐ a. It was bought in Peru.
   ☐ b. It was made of pure gold.
   ☐ c. It was never really lost at all.

2. We may assume that Mr. Merivale came to South Plains to
   ☐ a. improve his health.
   ☐ b. cheat the citizens there.
   ☐ c. make some lifelong friends.

3. Clues in the story suggest that Mr. Merivale and the bum
   ☐ a. never met each other.
   ☐ b. were the same person or partners.
   ☐ c. were very honest.

4. At the end of the story, how do you think Mike Brock, Cy Archer, Luke Williams, and Ben Woods felt?
   ☐ a. foolish and angry
   ☐ b. very happy
   ☐ c. amused

Thinking More About the Story

- The title of this selection is "The Lion Roared." It may be said that the gold lion in the story "roared" with laughter. Explain.
- In your opinion, who was the bum who appeared at the end of the story? Give reasons to support your answer.
- What things did Mr. Merivale do to make the citizens of South Plains fall for his scheme? (Think about Mr. Merivale's clothing and actions, as well as his words, in answering this question.)

Use the boxes below to total your scores for the exercises.

☐ +	**T**elling About the Story
☐ +	**W**atching for New Vocabulary Words
☐ +	**I**dentifying Story Elements
☐ +	**S**electing Words from the Story
☐ ▼	**T**hinking About the Story
☐	**S**core Total: Story 9

☐ × 5 = ☐

NUMBER CORRECT   YOUR SCORE

10. The Cage

by Martin Raim

There was no way out.

The walls of his cell were built of thick cement blocks. The huge door was made of steel. The floor and ceiling were made of concrete, and there were no windows. The only light came from a light bulb that was covered by a metal shield.

There was no way out, or so it seemed to him.

He had volunteered to be part of a scientific experiment and had been put in the cell to test the cleverness of the human mind. The cell was empty, and he was not allowed to take anything into it. But he had been told that there was *one* way to escape from the cell, and he had three hours to find it.

He began with the door. It stood before him, huge and gray. The three large hinges on the door were riveted into the wall and could not be removed. The door itself seemed too big for the small cell, and for a minute he wondered if it had been put up first and the rest of the cell built around it.

Finally he turned away from the door and looked around. He tried pushing against the cement blocks to see if any of them were loose. He searched the floor for a trap door. Then he glanced up at the ceiling. The shield! The shield around the light bulb! His mind raced. The metal shield could be used as a tool—the tool he needed! He had found the way to escape!

He moved under the shield and looked closely at it. One good strong pull would free it, he decided. He reached up, grabbed hold of it, and pulled. But the shield stayed attached to the ceiling. He grabbed the shield again, twisting it as he pulled. He felt it rip free, and he fell to the floor clutching his treasure.

The shield was shaped like a cone and had been fastened to the ceiling by three long metal prongs. These prongs were sharp. But they were not strong enough to cut through steel or concrete or cement.

He felt a hopelessness creep over him. He could find no use for the shield as a tool. The shield was not what he needed to get out.

Then he had a brilliant idea. True, the metal prongs of the shield could not cut through the steel door or the concrete floor or the cement blocks in the wall. But the prongs might be strong enough to dig out the mortar that held the cement blocks in place. He pulled off one of the prongs and scraped hard at the mortar. The mortar crumbled into powder. His idea worked! If he removed enough mortar, he could loosen a couple of the cement blocks, then push them out, and escape!

He selected two blocks near the door and set to work. The prong dug into the mortar and sent it flying out in a steady stream. The prong was just what he had needed. Now he was sure he would escape. But his hand made a sudden careless twist, and the metal prong broke into two useless pieces.

At first a wave of anger stunned him. Then he remembered that the shield had two more prongs. He pulled off another prong and went back to work. He decided he must be more careful—nothing must go wrong. There was still plenty of time left.

Soon he had chipped out four inches of mortar. But the jagged edges of the cement blocks had torn the skin off his knuckles. His hands were bleeding from a dozen burning cuts. His back and shoulders hurt from the strain of working in one position. The mortar dust blew into his eyes and down his throat. The work dragged on, slower and slower.

Suddenly the second prong broke.

For a minute he welcomed the excuse to stop working. But the thought of failure sent him back into action. He pulled off the third and last prong and went to work again. He was a man who did not like to lose—he had to win.

The work dragged on. He became numb to the pain in his hands, to the ache in his shoulders. His fingers moved blindly, and his attack against the mortar grew weaker and weaker.

At last he broke through. He had dug out enough mortar so that now he could see light between the cement blocks.

With a spurt of new energy he chipped away at the rest of the mortar. Of course there was a way out. He had found it, hadn't he? He had proved that a clever mind could solve any problem. That's how he had done it—with his own cleverness.

At that instant the third prong snapped in his hand.

He stared at the useless pieces. Then in a blind rage he slammed his fist against the wall.

Behind him the door of the cell opened slowly. His time had run out. His part in the experiment was over.

He was not allowed to talk about the experiment or about his plan of escape. However, he was sure that he could have escaped. He was convinced that he almost *had*.

Actually, he had not even come close.

The shield had been put around the light bulb only as a shade for the light. The metal prongs were not meant to be used as a tool.

The man had been clever, but he had let his cleverness sidetrack him. If he had not been so quick to use the shield as a tool, if he had not spent all his time chipping out the mortar, and if he had not stopped searching the cell, he might have found the real way out. He might have discovered that he could have left the cell as easily as he had entered.

For the huge door had never been locked.

TELLING ABOUT THE STORY. Complete each of the following statements by putting an *x* in the box next to the correct answer. Each statement tells something about the story.

1. The character in "The Cage" volunteered to
   □ a. spend several days in prison.
   □ b. take part in a scientific experiment.
   □ c. exchange places with another prisoner.

2. The man was told that
   □ a. he would probably be unable to escape from the cell.
   □ b. there was one way to escape from the cell.
   □ c. he could talk about his plan of escape later.

3. The prisoner thought that he could escape by
   □ a. loosening a couple of cement blocks and then pushing them out.
   □ b. finding a window and climbing through it.
   □ c. removing the hinges from the huge steel door.

4. At the end of the story, the prisoner believed that
   □ a. it was not possible to escape from the cell.
   □ b. he needed another week to escape.
   □ c. he had come close to escaping.

[ ] × 5 = [ ]

NUMBER
CORRECT

YOUR
SCORE

WATCHING FOR NEW VOCABULARY WORDS. Answer the following vocabulary questions by putting an *x* in the box next to the correct response.

1. The door of the cell was riveted into the wall and could not be removed. What is the meaning of the word *riveted*?
   □ a. pasted or glued
   □ b. bolted or fastened firmly
   □ c. painted or colored brightly

2. The prisoner used the prong on the metal shield as a tool. Which phrase best defines the word *prong*?
   □ a. a sharply pointed edge
   □ b. a heavy steel bar
   □ c. a hammer or ax

3. The mortar around the blocks crumbled into powder. Define the word *mortar*.
   □ a. paint
   □ b. wallpaper
   □ c. a mixture of cement, sand, and water

4. With a spurt of new energy, the prisoner began working again. What is the meaning of the word *spurt*?
   □ a. sudden burst
   □ b. loss
   □ c. payment

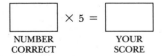

[ ] × 5 = [ ]

NUMBER
CORRECT

YOUR
SCORE

IDENTIFYING STORY ELEMENTS. Each of the following questions tests your understanding of story elements. Put an *x* in the box next to each correct answer.

1. What is the *setting* of "The Cage"?
   ☐ a. a prison courtyard
   ☐ b. a warden's office
   ☐ c. a cell

2. What happened first in the *plot* of the story?
   ☐ a. The prisoner reached up and grabbed the metal shield around the light bulb.
   ☐ b. The door of the cell opened slowly.
   ☐ c. The prisoner saw light between the cement blocks.

3. Which statement best describes the main *character* in the story?
   ☐ a. He gave up easily.
   ☐ b. He was a coward.
   ☐ c. He hated to lose.

4. Identify the sentence which best expresses the *theme* of "The Cage."
   ☐ a. It is a bad idea to volunteer for an experiment.
   ☐ b. Sometimes, it is difficult to see what is right before one's eyes.
   ☐ c. Crime does not pay.

SELECTING WORDS FROM THE STORY. Complete the following paragraph by filling in each blank with one of the words listed below. Each of the words appears in the story. Since there are five words and four blanks, one word in the group will not be used.

According to an old tale, the Minotaur was a monster which lived on _____ (1) flesh. It was kept in a _____ (2) maze in Crete. The maze had so many different tricky paths, no one who was placed in it was able to _____ (3) . Theseus unwound a ball of string as he _____ (4) through the maze. He killed the monster, then followed the string path to freedom.

human   went

ceiling

huge   escape

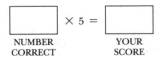

NUMBER CORRECT × 5 = YOUR SCORE

NUMBER CORRECT × 5 = YOUR SCORE

THINKING ABOUT THE STORY. Each of the following questions requires you to think critically about the selection. Put an *x* in the box next to the correct answer.

1. The prisoner didn't realize that
   - ☐ a. it was impossible to get out of the cell.
   - ☐ b. there was a trap door hidden in the floor.
   - ☐ c. he could have escaped from the cell by opening the door.

2. Probably, the prisoner didn't try to leave by the door because he
   - ☐ a. had been told not to.
   - ☐ b. knew the door was locked.
   - ☐ c. was looking for a more difficult method of escaping.

3. The story suggests that what is obvious is
   - ☐ a. often difficult to find.
   - ☐ b. usually wrong.
   - ☐ c. usually right.

4. The story seems to suggest that the prisoner failed to escape because he
   - ☐ a. didn't try hard enough.
   - ☐ b. was *too* clever.
   - ☐ c. needed just a few more hours.

Thinking More About the Story

- Suppose that the prisoner had *another* three hours to figure out how to escape. Do you think he would have succeeded? Explain.
- The purpose of the experiment was to test the cleverness of the human mind. Based on the prisoner's actions, what are some conclusions that might be drawn?
- Suppose that the same experiment was repeated with many other prisoners. Do you think most would have acted the way this prisoner did? Or do you think that the majority would have escaped through the unlocked door? Explain your answer.

Use the boxes below to total your scores for the exercises.

☐ +	**T**elling About the Story
☐ +	**W**atching for New Vocabulary Words
☐ +	**I**dentifying Story Elements
☐ +	**S**electing Words from the Story
☐ ▼	**T**hinking About the Story
☐	**S**core Total: Story 10

☐ × 5 = ☐

NUMBER   YOUR
CORRECT   SCORE

11. Two Were Left

by Hugh B. Cave

On the third night of hunger, Noni thought of the dog. Nothing lived upon that floating island of ice except himself and the dog.

When the ice broke up, Noni had lost his sled, his food, his furs, even his knife. He had saved only Nimuk, his great devoted husky. And now the two, completely alone, marooned on the ice, eyed each other warily.

Noni's love for Nimuk was real, very real. It was as real as hunger and cold nights and the gnawing pain of his injured leg. But the men of his village killed their dogs when food was scarce, didn't they? And they killed them without thinking about it twice.

He told himself that Nimuk, when hungry enough, would begin to seek food. "One of us will soon be devouring the other," Noni thought. "So . . ."

He could not kill the dog with his bare

hands. Nimuk was powerful and much less tired than he. A weapon, then, was needed.

Noni took off his mittens and unstrapped the brace from his injured leg. When he had hurt his leg a few weeks before, he had made the brace from bits of harness and two thin strips of iron.

He kneeled and wedged one of the iron strips into a crack in the ice. Then he began to rub the other iron strip against it with firm, slow strokes.

Nimuk watched him, and it seemed to Noni that the dog's eyes glowed more brightly.

He kept working, trying not to remember why. The strip of iron had an edge now. It had begun to take shape. By daylight his task was completed. He had finished making a knife!

Noni pulled the knife from the ice and felt its edge. The sun's glare reflected from it. Its brightness stabbed at his eyes and, for an instant, blinded him momentarily.

Noni forced himself to call the dog.

"Here, Nimuk!" he called softly.

The dog suspiciously watched him.

"Come here," Noni called.

Nimuk came closer. Noni saw fear in the animal's gaze. He could see hunger and suffering in the dog's labored breathing and awkward movements. Noni's heart wept. He hated himself and fought against it.

Closer Nimuk came, aware of Noni's intentions. Now Noni felt a thickening in his throat. He saw the dog's eyes, and they were pools of suffering.

Now! Now was the time to strike!

A great sob shook Noni's kneeling body. He cursed the knife. He swayed blindly and threw the knife far away from him. With empty hands outstretched, he stumbled toward the dog and fell.

The dog growled as he circled the boy's body. And now Noni was sick with fear.

In flinging away the knife, he had left himself defenseless. He was too weak to crawl after it now. He was at Nimuk's mercy. And Nimuk was hungry.

The dog had circled him and was creeping up from behind him. Noni heard a rattle in the animal's throat.

Noni shut his eyes, praying that the attack might be swift. He felt the dog's feet against his leg, the hot rush of Nimuk's breath against his neck. A scream gathered in the boy's throat.

Then he felt the dog's hot tongue licking his face.

Noni's eyes opened. Crying softly, he thrust out an arm and drew the dog's head down against his own.

The plane came out of the south an hour later. Its pilot was a young man in the coast patrol. He looked down and saw the large floating iceberg. And he saw something flashing.

The sun was gleaming off something shiny, which moved. His curiosity aroused, the pilot circled and flew lower. Now he saw, in the shadow of the mountain of ice, a dark, still shape that appeared to be human. Or were there two shapes?

He set his seaplane down on the water and investigated. There were two shapes, a boy and a dog. The boy was unconscious but alive. The dog whined feebly but was too weak to move.

The gleaming object which had caught the pilot's attention was a crudely-made knife. It was stuck, point down, into the ice a short distance away, and was quivering in the wind.

TELLING ABOUT THE STORY. Complete each of the following statements by putting an *x* in the box next to the correct answer. Each statement tells something about the story.

1. At the beginning of the story, Noni thought that
   ☐ a. he and Nimuk would be rescued by the coast patrol.
   ☐ b. he would kill Nimuk, or Nimuk would kill him.
   ☐ c. the men of his village would send food.

2. When the ice broke up, Noni saved his
   ☐ a. sled.
   ☐ b. furs.
   ☐ c. dog.

3. Noni used the thin strips of iron to
   ☐ a. build a fire.
   ☐ b. make a knife.
   ☐ c. leave a signal for a passing plane.

4. The pilot's attention was first drawn to
   ☐ a. a shiny object that gleamed in the sun.
   ☐ b. two figures on the ice.
   ☐ c. the barking of the husky.

WATCHING FOR NEW VOCABULARY WORDS. Answer the following vocabulary questions by putting an *x* in the box next to the correct response.

1. Noni and Nimuk eyed each other warily. Which phrase best defines the word *warily?*
   ☐ a. in a careful or cautious manner
   ☐ b. in a pleased or happy way
   ☐ c. in a tired or exhausted condition

2. The two were completely alone, marooned on the island of ice. The word *marooned* means
   ☐ a. abandoned or separated from others.
   ☐ b. very cold or frozen.
   ☐ c. extremely hungry or starving.

3. The sun's glare blinded him momentarily. What is the meaning of the word *momentarily?*
   ☐ a. for a long period of time
   ☐ b. for a brief period of time
   ☐ c. with great harm

4. Nimuk slowly crawled closer, aware of Noni's intentions. Define the word *intentions.*
   ☐ a. worries
   ☐ b. injuries
   ☐ c. plans

	× 5 =	
NUMBER CORRECT		**YOUR SCORE**

	× 5 =	
NUMBER CORRECT		**YOUR SCORE**

IDENTIFYING STORY ELEMENTS. Each of the following questions tests your understanding of story elements. Put an *x* in the box next to each correct answer.

1. What is the *setting* of "Two Were Left"?
   ☐ a. a lake
   ☐ b. an iceberg
   ☐ c. a large island in the Pacific Ocean

2. What happened last in the *plot* of the story?
   ☐ a. Noni called softly to Nimuk.
   ☐ b. The pilot circled the plane and flew lower.
   ☐ c. Nimuk licked Noni's face.

3. Which word best describes the *mood* of "Two Were Left"?
   ☐ a. cheerful
   ☐ b. humorous
   ☐ c. suspenseful

4. Identify the statement which best expresses the *theme* of the story.
   ☐ a. Everyone should have a pet.
   ☐ b. Sometimes, love can be its own reward.
   ☐ c. A hungry animal is often very dangerous.

SELECTING WORDS FROM THE STORY. Complete the following paragraph by filling in each blank with one of the words listed below. Each of the words appears in the story. Since there are five words and four blanks, one word in the group will not be used.

A large group of Eskimos has gathered

along the _____ of Alaska.
                        1

Food is not as _____ in this
                          2

area as it is in other parts of the far North.

Probably, for this reason, Alaskan Eskimos

have decided to establish permanent

_____ there. Like most Eskimos
        3

today, Alaskan Eskimos _____
                                      4

in wooden houses rather than in igloos.

scarce   coast

villages

live   nights

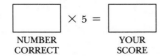

NUMBER   YOUR
CORRECT   SCORE

× 5 =

NUMBER   YOUR
CORRECT   SCORE

THINKING ABOUT THE STORY. Each of the following questions requires you to think critically about the selection. Put an *x* in the box next to the correct answer.

1. Why did Noni sway and throw the knife blindly away?
   - ☐ a. He was weak from hunger.
   - ☐ b. He couldn't bring himself to attack the dog.
   - ☐ c. He was confused because of the bitter cold.

2. At one point in the story, Noni became sick with fear. Probably, he felt that way because he
   - ☐ a. realized that he was going to die of hunger.
   - ☐ b. thought that Nimuk was going to attack him.
   - ☐ c. knew that his injured leg was getting worse.

3. We may infer that if Noni had attacked Nimuk with the knife, then
   - ☐ a. Nimuk would have managed to escape from him.
   - ☐ b. Nimuk would have killed Noni.
   - ☐ c. the pilot would not have found them.

4. What probably happened to Noni and Nimuk?
   - ☐ a. They were rescued by the pilot.
   - ☐ b. They died before they could be rescued.
   - ☐ c. They never trusted each other again.

	× 5 =	
NUMBER CORRECT		YOUR SCORE

Thinking More About the Story

- At the beginning of "Two Were Left," there is evidence that Nimuk knew that Noni was planning to attack. Still, the dog came closer when called. Why?
- Suppose that Noni had attacked Nimuk with his crudely-made knife. What do you think would have happened? How might the story have ended?
- Sometimes, a story offers a lesson, or moral. What lesson, or lessons, can be drawn from this story?

Use the boxes below to total your scores for the exercises.

☐ +	**T**elling About the Story
☐ +	**W**atching for New Vocabulary Words
☐ +	**I**dentifying Story Elements
☐ +	**S**electing Words from the Story
☐ ▼	**T**hinking About the Story
☐	**S**core Total: Story 11

12. The Precious Stones of Axolotyl

by Manuela Williams Crosno

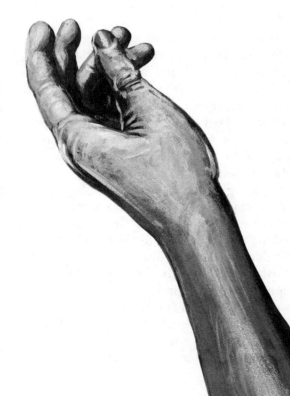

Once long ago, there was an old woman who lived near the village of Agua Clara, which means "clear water." Although she was to live for many years more, she seemed older than anyone in the village. No one could remember where she came from or when.

She lived in a small lean-to built against a great rock. Among her few possessions were a herd of goats and an oddly shaped stick on which it was her custom to lean heavily as she went about her work.

She was so wrinkled one could not see her eyes to tell what color they were. Her skin was deep brown, like pine cones when they fall to the ground. And when she laughed she showed just two teeth. Because no one knew her name, and because she seemed to have lived in the mountains from their very beginning, she was called "La Vieja de las montañas"—the old woman of the mountains.

Now there resided in the village of Agua Clara three small boys whose names were Anselmo, Felipe, and Guillermo. They lived in separate houses built of adobe. The houses were almost as alike as the boys, who were the same age and were constant companions.

One time when they went toward the mountains, they came upon the goats of La Vieja, unwatched, and eating peacefully at the sparse gramma grass that grew about. Guillermo began to throw stones at the animals. Anselmo howled like a coyote. Felipe gave the weird cry of the mountain lion. The goats, in a panic, began to run in all directions.

Suddenly, the voice of La Vieja called to them. The goats stopped where they were and again ate grass in a peaceful manner. The boys turned homeward, but standing in their pathway and leaning on her stick was La Vieja.

Shaking her stick in his direction, she said to Anselmo, "You howled like a coyote to frighten my goats. You are unwise." And to Guillermo, "You threw stones to hurt my goats. You are unkind." Then to Felipe, "You cried like the lion of the mountains to make my goats run away. You have little understanding." To all three she said, "When you have learned wisdom, kindness, and understanding, then I will show you the precious stones of axolotyl."

Stepping aside, she disappeared behind a rock, leaving the boys somewhat frightened. For many days they thought about this meeting with La Vieja, and they *never forgot* the words of the old woman.

Many years passed and Guillermo, Anselmo, and Felipe grew to manhood. Anselmo was judge of all disputes in the village and was considered to be very wise. However, if anyone had a story to tell and needed a sympathetic ear, he went to Felipe who could always be counted upon for understanding. Guillermo was the one to call when a child was hurt, for he ministered to the ill and needy. It was well known in the village that no one was as kind

and as gentle as Guillermo.

Now when Otero became governor, he sent his soldiers about the country to seize any possessions of value which they might discover. They had heard of the precious stones of axolotyl which were said to belong to La Vieja, and although the soldiers thought this talk was probably just a fable, they went to the old woman.

"We have come for your jewels!" they said.

She was silent for a long moment. Then she smiled—a smile they could not interpret. It showed her two teeth, but since they could not see her eyes, they did not know whether or not she was angry.

"They are the jewels of axolotyl, the water dog," she said, finally. "Come with me and I will show them to you."

The soldiers followed La Vieja past the place where the goats were coralled, and beyond her house into the wooded foothills. She walked slowly and leaned heavily on her stick. Finally, she came to a pool beyond a waterfall where it seemed the waters, after their noisy dash over the rocks, had stopped to rest. There was no movement in the still depths of the pool. Glistening far below the surface were rocks of many colors.

"See the green one?" she asked, pointing to a green pebble near the bottom of the pool. "See the scarlet one," she said, selecting a red pebble still farther in the clear depths. "See the perfectly white one?" she asked, thrusting the stick toward the deepest part of the pool. The soldiers nodded and looked at one another.

"Those," she cried, laughing triumphantly, "are the precious stones of axolotyl!"

Now axolotyl is a water dog and is

reported to be poisonous. Long ago, it is said, he took the soul of one of the people. So the soldiers were afraid of him or the mention of his name. They looked at the rocks shining in the pool. They looked at La Vieja.

"She is a foolish old woman," they whispered together. "These are not precious stones, they are but rocks."

Since she had no jewels, and because they felt that she had attempted to deceive them, the soldiers took La Vieja to Agua Clara. There she was locked in a small room where she was to remain for many days. After some time, there was a knock at her door and Felipe stood outside. He had heard that she was ill and had come with food. She would accept nothing, however. Instead, she said these words which she repeated many times:

"You understand, amigo, you understand."

Still later, there was a voice at her window in the dark and Guillermo whispered, "La Viejita, I have cared for your goats and brought you your walking stick which I found near the corral."

She remembered where the soldiers had thrown her stick and she accepted it gratefully. For a long time she looked at Guillermo in the darkness until she recognized who he was. Then she said, "Amigo, you are kind—very kind."

Finally, Anselmo pleaded with the governor to let the woman go because she was old and owned no precious stones. The governor would not permit La Vieja to be freed until Anselmo had promised him many pesos to help pay for the soldiers.

The old woman of the mountains thanked Anselmo for her release, and said to him,

"Amigo mio, I see that you are one who is very wise. Tomorrow, bring Felipe and Guillermo with you and come to see me."

Since he wished to please her, Anselmo called his friends the next day. Together they went to the place where La Vieja was tending her goats. She smiled when she saw the three friends and said, "You have indeed learned wisdom and kindness and understanding. Come with me."

Slowly she led them to the pool which was bathed in sunlight and shadow. It was the pool she had shown the soldiers. Pointing to the three stones shining within it, she said, "These are the precious stones of axolotyl."

Now she took the long stick on which she had always leaned so heavily, and turned the knob outward. They saw that it was a cup which swiveled, and that when the stick was turned about, it resembled a large dipper. Thus, she thrust the stick into the pool once and brought up the white stone, and gave it to Anselmo saying, "For wisdom." In the same manner she dipped the stick into the pool again, and gave the green stone to Guillermo, telling him only that he had become very kind. Again the stick went into the water and this time the red stone was placed in the hand of Felipe, "For understanding."

Soon after this, La Vieja died, but she was never forgotten. Felipe, Guillermo, and Anselmo carried the stones in their pockets for some time before they learned that one was a diamond, another an emerald, and the third one, a ruby. Yet they never considered them as priceless as the real jewels of axolotyl.

TELLING ABOUT THE STORY. Complete each of the following statements by putting an *x* in the box next to the correct answer. Each statement tells something about the story.

1. La Vieja told the boys that when they learned wisdom, kindness, and understanding, she would
   ☐ a. make them very wealthy.
   ☐ b. help them find jobs in the village.
   ☐ c. show them the precious stones of axolotyl.

2. The soldiers ordered La Vieja to hand over her
   ☐ a. jewels.
   ☐ b. money.
   ☐ c. goats.

3. Anselmo gained La Vieja's release by
   ☐ a. helping her break out of the room in which she was locked.
   ☐ b. pleading with the governor and promising him many pesos.
   ☐ c. proving that she was innocent of any crime.

4. La Vieja used her long stick to
   ☐ a. fight off the soldiers.
   ☐ b. dip stones from the pool.
   ☐ c. chase the goats into the corral.

WATCHING FOR NEW VOCABULARY WORDS. Answer the following vocabulary questions by putting an *x* in the box next to the correct response.

1. The three boys resided in the village of Agua Clara. Define the word *resided*.
   ☐ a. argued
   ☐ b. lived
   ☐ c. traveled

2. Anselmo, who was very wise, was judge of all disputes in the village. Which word or phrase best defines *disputes*?
   ☐ a. quarrels or differences of opinion
   ☐ b. visitors or guests
   ☐ c. officers or soldiers

3. The kind and gentle Guillermo ministered to the ill and needy. As used in this sentence, the word *ministered* means
   ☐ a. served as an agent of the government.
   ☐ b. offered aid or assistance.
   ☐ c. acted harshly.

4. Felipe, who could always be counted on for understanding, had a sympathetic ear. A person who is *sympathetic*
   ☐ a. spends much time listening to music.
   ☐ b. doesn't care about others.
   ☐ c. shows kind feelings to others.

☐ × 5 = ☐
NUMBER CORRECT   YOUR SCORE

☐ × 5 = ☐
NUMBER CORRECT   YOUR SCORE

IDENTIFYING STORY ELEMENTS. Each of the following questions tests your understanding of story elements. Put an *x* in the box next to each correct answer.

1. Where is "The Precious Stones of Axolotyl" *set?*
   ☐ a. in a large city in Mexico
   ☐ b. in a prison in Spain
   ☐ c. in and around the village of Agua Clara

2. What happened first in the *plot* of the story?
   ☐ a. La Vieja was locked in a small room.
   ☐ b. The boys scared La Vieja's goats.
   ☐ c. La Vieja gave a green stone to Guillermo.

3. Which sentence best *characterizes* La Vieja?
   ☐ a. She was old and wise.
   ☐ b. She was very lazy.
   ☐ c. She didn't care about anybody but herself.

4. Identify the statement which best expresses the *theme* of the story.
   ☐ a. Wisdom, kindness, and understanding are rewarded.
   ☐ b. Precious stones are more valuable than anything.
   ☐ c. Mountain pools sometime contain valuable jewels.

SELECTING WORDS FROM THE STORY. Complete the following paragraph by filling in each blank with one of the words listed below. Each of the words appears in the story. Since there are five words and four blanks, one word in the group will not be used.

Francisco Vasquez de Coronado set off on what proved to be a disappointing journey. Indians who had been _____ by Coronado's soldiers told tales of cities which glistened in the sun. These cities, they said, were filled with gold and other _____ metals. Coronado and his men _____ to discover these cities. But all they found were _____ pueblos in the broiling deserts of Arizona and New Mexico.

seized   wisdom

attempted

adobe   precious

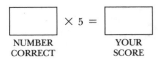

NUMBER CORRECT   × 5 =   YOUR SCORE

NUMBER CORRECT   × 5 =   YOUR SCORE

THINKING ABOUT THE STORY. Each of the following questions requires you to think critically about the selection. Put an *x* in the box next to the correct answer.

1. Evidence in the story indicates that Anselmo, Felipe, and Guillermo
   ☐ a. did not care about La Vieja.
   ☐ b. listened to La Vieja.
   ☐ c. were very selfish.

2. Which one of the following statements is true?
   ☐ a. The soldiers thought all along that La Vieja was wealthy.
   ☐ b. The boys realized at once that the stones given to them were worth much money.
   ☐ c. La Vieja taught the boys an important lesson.

3. Clues in the story suggest that the characters speak
   ☐ a. Spanish.
   ☐ b. French.
   ☐ c. German.

4. Read the last sentence of the story again. What were the "real" jewels of axolotyl?
   ☐ a. three pebbles which did not have much value
   ☐ b. a diamond, an emerald, and a ruby
   ☐ c. the qualities of wisdom, kindness, and understanding

☐ × 5 = ☐

NUMBER   YOUR
CORRECT   SCORE

Thinking More About the Story

- "The Precious Stones of Axolotyl" seems to offer the reader a lesson, or moral. What lesson, or lessons, are suggested by the story?
- When the soldiers demanded La Vieja's jewels, she took the officers to the pool, where she pointed out the shining stones. Why didn't the soldiers believe her? Do you think that La Vieja knew all along that the soldiers would not listen to her? Explain.
- What might Anselmo, Felipe, and Guillermo have told their own children about "La Vieja de las montañas"—the old woman of the mountains?

Use the boxes below to total your scores for the exercises.

☐
+
Telling About the Story

☐
+
Watching for New Vocabulary Words

☐
+
Identifying Story Elements

☐
+
Selecting Words from the Story

☐
▼
Thinking About the Story

☐
Score Total: Story 12

13. **The Immortal Bard**

by Isaac Asimov

"Oh, yes," said Dr. Phineas Welch, "I can bring back the spirits of famous people who have died."

Scott Robertson, the school's young English instructor, adjusted his glasses. He looked to the right and the left to see if they were being overheard. "Really, Dr. Welch," he said.

"I mean it," said the scientist. "And not just the spirits. I can bring back the bodies, too."

"I wouldn't have thought it were possible," said Robertson.

"Why not? It's just a matter of temporal transference."

"You mean *time travel?* But that's quite— uh—unusual."

"Not if you know how."

"Well, then how, Dr. Welch?"

"Sorry," said the scientist. "I can't tell you that." He looked around vaguely, then said, "But I have brought quite a few back. Archimides. Newton. Galileo. Poor fellows."

"Didn't they like it here? I should think they'd have been fascinated by our modern science," said the English teacher. He was beginning to enjoy the conversation.

"Oh, they were. They were. At first. Especially Archimides. He was delighted after I explained a little of it using some Greek I'd learned. But no—no—"

"What was wrong?"

"They couldn't get used to our way of life. Our culture is so different. They got terribly lonely and frightened. I had to send them back."

"That's too bad."

"Yes. Great minds, but not flexible minds. Not universal, for all time. So I tried Shakespeare."

"*What?*" yelled the English teacher. This was getting closer to home.

"Don't yell, my boy," said Welch. "It's bad manners."

"Did you say you brought back William Shakespeare—the greatest writer who ever lived!"

"I did. I needed someone with a universal mind, someone who understood people well enough to be able to live with them centuries after his own time. Shakespeare was the man. I've got his signature. As a souvenir, you know."

"Do you have it with you?" asked Robertson, his eyes growing wide.

"It's right here." Welch fumbled in one vest pocket after another. "Ah, here it is," he said.

Welch passed a small slip of paper to the instructor. On it, in jagged, uneven script was written: William Shakespeare.

"What did he look like?" Robertson asked eagerly.

"Not like his pictures. Bald with an ugly mustache. He spoke in a thick accent. Of course, I did my best to please him. I told him we thought highly of his plays and still performed them. In fact, I said we thought they were the greatest works of literature in the English language, maybe in any language."

"Good. Good," said the English teacher breathlessly.

"I said that people had written many books about his plays. Naturally he wanted to see one, and I got one for him from the library."

"What did he think?"

"Oh, he was fascinated. Of course, he had some trouble with some of our current expressions and with references to events after the year 1600. But I helped out. Poor fellow. I don't think he ever expected to receive so much attention for his writing. He kept saying over and over, 'Have mercy, upon my word.' "

The scientist thought for a moment. "Then I told him that we even give college courses in Shakespeare."

"*I* teach a course in Shakespeare," said Robertson.

"I know. I enrolled him in the evening class you give, 'The Works of Shakespeare.' I never saw a man as eager as Bill to find out what others thought of him. He worked hard in your class."

"You enrolled William Shakespeare in

my class?" mumbled Robertson. The thought stunned him. Was it possible? Could William Shakespeare have been his student? He was beginning to recall a bald man with a funny way of talking. . . .

"I didn't enroll him under his real name, of course," said Dr. Welch. "Never mind what name he used. It was a mistake, that's all. A big mistake. Poor fellow." He shook his head sadly.

"Why was it a mistake?" asked Robertson. "What happened?"

"I had to send him back to his own time," said Welch, angrily. "How much shame do you think a man can stand?"

"What shame are you talking about?" asked the English teacher.

Dr. Welch stared at him. "What shame? Why, my dear fellow, you *failed* him!"

TELLING ABOUT THE STORY. Complete each of the following statements by putting an *x* in the box next to the correct answer. Each statement tells something about the story.

1. Dr. Phineas Welch stated that he could
   - ☐ a. teach an evening class in Shakespeare.
   - ☐ b. travel into the future.
   - ☐ c. bring back people who had died.

2. William Shakespeare was eager to
   - ☐ a. find out what others thought of his writings.
   - ☐ b. discuss modern science with Dr. Welch.
   - ☐ c. let everyone know who he was.

3. Scott Robertson was surprised to discover that Shakespeare
   - ☐ a. looked just like his pictures.
   - ☐ b. expected to receive much attention.
   - ☐ c. had been a student in his class.

4. Shakespeare was sent back to his own time because he
   - ☐ a. got terribly lonely.
   - ☐ b. couldn't stand the shame of failing Robertson's class.
   - ☐ c. couldn't get used to our modern language.

WATCHING FOR NEW VOCABULARY WORDS. Answer the following vocabulary questions by putting an *x* in the box next to the correct response.

1. Scott Robertson was the school's young English instructor. What is the meaning of the word *instructor?*
   - ☐ a. scientist
   - ☐ b. doctor
   - ☐ c. teacher

2. According to Dr. Welch, people who lived long ago had trouble adjusting to our culture. Which of the following phrases best defines the word *culture?*
   - ☐ a. the customs, art, and beliefs of a society
   - ☐ b. methods of transportation and communication
   - ☐ c. different kinds of music

3. Dr. Welch enrolled Shakespeare in Scott Robertson's evening class at the school. Define the word *enrolled.*
   - ☐ a. registered or entered
   - ☐ b. questioned or asked
   - ☐ c. hired or employed

4. William Shakespeare's signature was written in jagged, uneven script. The word *jagged* means
   - ☐ a. smooth and level.
   - ☐ b. rough or ragged.
   - ☐ c. very neat.

	× 5 =	
NUMBER CORRECT		YOUR SCORE

	× 5 =	
NUMBER CORRECT		YOUR SCORE

86

IDENTIFYING STORY ELEMENTS. Each of the following questions tests your understanding of story elements. Put an *x* in the box next to each correct answer.

1. What happened last in the *plot* of the story?
   ☐ a. Dr. Welch showed Robertson a slip of paper with Shakespeare's signature on it.
   ☐ b. Robertson remembered a bald man who was a student in his class.
   ☐ c. Robertson looked around to see if they were being overheard.

2. Which of the following phrases best *characterizes* Shakespeare?
   ☐ a. a remarkable scientist
   ☐ b. the author of ordinary plays
   ☐ c. a truly great writer

3. Identify the phrase which best describes the author's *purpose* in writing the story.
   ☐ a. to tell or inform the reader about William Shakespeare
   ☐ b. to convince the reader that Shakespeare was a great writer
   ☐ c. to amuse and entertain the reader

4. Which sentence best describes the *style* of "The Immortal Bard"?
   ☐ a. It contains numerous descriptive passages.
   ☐ b. It is told mainly through dialogue.
   ☐ c. It has many long and difficult passages.

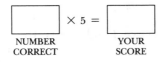

NUMBER CORRECT × 5 = YOUR SCORE

SELECTING WORDS FROM THE STORY. Complete the following paragraph by filling in each blank with one of the words listed below. Each of the words appears in the story. Since there are five words and four blanks, one word in the group will not be used.

The plays of William Shakespeare have always _____ and delighted audiences. Although they were written about four _____ ago, they still remain fresh and exciting. In all, Shakespeare wrote thirty-eight plays. They have been translated into many _____ , and have been performed all over the world. Shakespeare is truly one of the best loved _____ of all time.

unusual   writers

centuries

languages   fascinated

NUMBER CORRECT × 5 = YOUR SCORE

THINKING ABOUT THE STORY. Each of the following questions requires you to think critically about the selection. Put an *x* in the box next to the correct answer.

1. Probably, the most amusing part of the story is that
   - ☐ a. Scott Robertson didn't realize that William Shakespeare was one of his students.
   - ☐ b. William Shakespeare spoke with a funny accent.
   - ☐ c. William Shakespeare failed a class in Shakespeare.

2. We may infer that Dr. Welch knew the secret of time travel because
   - ☐ a. he was a scientist.
   - ☐ b. he learned it from Archimides, Newton, or Galileo.
   - ☐ c. Scott Robertson shared the secret with him.

3. At the end of the story, Scott Robertson probably felt
   - ☐ a. very pleased with himself.
   - ☐ b. very foolish.
   - ☐ c. proud to have met William Shakespeare.

4. Most likely, this story takes place
   - ☐ a. on a spaceship.
   - ☐ b. in a school.
   - ☐ c. at a sports event.

[ ] × 5 = [ ]

NUMBER   YOUR
CORRECT   SCORE

Thinking More About the Story

- Why did Dr. Phineas Welch think that William Shakespeare was the perfect person to "bring back"? In view of what happened in the story, do you think that Dr. Welch changed his mind? Explain.
- Suppose that Scott Robertson had realized that the bald man in his class was William Shakespeare. Would Robertson have acted differently? If so, in what ways? How might the story have then ended?
- If William Shakespeare could visit our present society for a week, what things do you think would astonish him most? Which would he find most pleasing? Most disappointing? Give reasons for your answers.

Use the boxes below to total your scores for the exercises.

[ ] **T**elling About the Story

[ ] **W**atching for New Vocabulary Words

[ ] **I**dentifying Story Elements

[ ] **S**electing Words from the Story

[ ] **T**hinking About the Story

[ ] **S**core Total: Story 13

14. Appointment at Noon

by Eric Frank Russell

*H*enry Curran was a big man, busy and successful. He had the build of a wrestler and the soul of a tiger. He had no patience for trifles. His time was worth a thousand bucks an hour. He knew of nobody who was worth more.

And crime did not pay? "Bah!" said Henry Curran. He believed that jungle methods paid off. He sneered at those who played by civilized rules.

Curran entered his spacious office with the swift, powerful steps of a large man in fighting condition. He threw his hat onto a hook, glanced at the clock on the wall, and noted that it was ten minutes to twelve.

He planted himself in the seat behind his desk and kept his gaze upon the door through which he had entered. His wait lasted about ten seconds. Scowling, Curran reached over and pushed a red button on his big desk.

"What's wrong with you?" he snapped when Miss Reed came in. "You get worse every day. Old age creeping over you or something?"

She paused, tall and neat, and faced him across the desk. Her eyes showed a touch of fear. Curran employed only those about whom he knew too much.

"I'm sorry, Mr. Curran, I was—"

"Never mind the alibi. Be faster—or else! Speed's what I like. *Speed*—see?"

"Yes, Mr. Curran."

"Has Lolordo phoned in yet?"

"No, Mr. Curran."

"He should be calling any moment now if everything went all right." Curran viewed the clock again, and tapped impatiently on his desk. "If he's made a mess of it and the lawyer phones, tell him to let Lolordo stew. He's in no position to talk, anyway. A stretch in jail will teach him not to be stupid."

"Yes, Mr. Curran. There's an old—"

"Quiet till I've finished. If Michaelson calls us and says the deal went through, ring Voss right away and tell him that without delay! And I mean without delay! That's important." He thought for a moment. "Now there's that meeting downtown at twelve-twenty I've got to get to. Nobody knows how long it will go on, but if they want trouble I can give it to them. If anyone asks, you don't know where I am and you don't expect me back before four."

"But, Mr. Curran—"

"You heard what I said. Nobody sees me before four."

"There's a man here already," she managed to say breathlessly. "He said you have an appointment with him at two minutes to twelve."

"And you fell for a line like that?" He looked at her with annoyance.

"I'm only repeating what he said. He seemed quite sincere."

"Sincere?" scoffed Curran. "In *my* office? He's got the wrong address. Go tell him to take a walk on some railroad tracks."

"I said you were out and didn't know when you would return. He took a seat and said he'd wait because you would be back at exactly ten to twelve."

Both stared at the clock. Curran bent an arm and looked at his wristwatch to check the accuracy of the clock on the wall.

"That's what I call a lucky guess," he said. "One minute either way would have made him wrong. Anyway, get him out—or do I have to get some of the boys to do it for you?"

"That won't be necessary. He is old and blind."

"That's *his* tough luck. Get him out!"

Obediently she left. A few moments later she was back with the pained look of one forced to face his anger.

"I'm terribly sorry, Mr. Curran, but he insists that he has a date with you for two minutes to twelve. He says he must see you about a matter of major importance."

Curran scowled at the wall. The clock said four minutes to twelve. He spoke loudly, with emphasis.

"I know no blind man. And I don't forget appointments. Now get him out at once."

She hesitated, standing there wide-eyed. "I'm wondering whether . . . whether . . ."

"Yes?"

"Whether he's been sent to you by someone, someone who didn't want him to be able to identify you by sight."

He thought it over and said, "Could be. You use your brains once in a while. What's his name?"

"He won't say."

"Did he state his business?"

"No."

"H'm! I'll give him two minutes. If he's looking for a handout for some charity, he'll go out through the window. Tell him time is precious and show him in."

She went away. A moment later, she brought back the visitor and gave him a chair. The door closed quietly behind her. The clock said three minutes before the hour.

Curran leaned back and looked closely at his visitor. He found him tall, thin, gaunt, and white-haired. The old man was dressed completely in black, a deep, solemn black that accented the brightness of the blue, unseeing eyes which stared from his colorless face.

Those strange eyes were the man's most striking feature. They possessed a very curious quality, as if they could look *into* the things they could not look *at*. And they were sorry—sorry for what they saw.

For the first time in his life, Curran felt a faint note of alarm. Curran said, "What can I do for you?"

"Nothing," replied the other. "Nothing at all."

His low voice was no louder than a whisper. With its sound, a strange coldness came over the room. He sat there unmoving and staring at whatever a blind man can see. The coldness increased and became bitter. Curran shivered despite himself. He scowled and got a hold on himself.

"Don't take up my time," advised Curran. "State your business or get out."

"People don't take up time. Time takes up people."

"What do you mean? Who are you?"

"You know who I am. Every man is a shining sun until dimmed by his dark companion."

"You're not funny," said Curran, freezing.

"I am never funny."

The tiger light blazed in Curran's eyes. He stood up and placed a thick, firm finger near the button on his desk.

"Enough of this nonsense! What d'you want?"

Suddenly extending a lengthless arm, Death whispered sadly, "You!"

And took him.

At exactly two minutes to twelve.

TELLING ABOUT THE STORY. Complete each of the following statements by putting an *x* in the box next to the correct answer. Each statement tells something about the story.

1. To Henry Curran, the most important thing was
   ☐ a. treating everyone fairly.
   ☐ b. keeping himself in good condition.
   ☐ c. having things done in a speedy way.

2. At first, Curran refused to see his visitor because
   ☐ a. Curran was afraid of the visitor.
   ☐ b. the visitor didn't have an appointment.
   ☐ c. Curran owed the visitor money.

3. Curran's visitor was
   ☐ a. blind.
   ☐ b. youthful.
   ☐ c. short.

4. Death took Henry Curran at exactly
   ☐ a. ten minutes to twelve.
   ☐ b. two minutes to twelve.
   ☐ c. four o'clock.

WATCHING FOR NEW VOCABULARY WORDS. Answer the following vocabulary questions by putting an *x* in the box next to the correct response.

1. Henry Curran looked at his wristwatch to check the accuracy of the clock on the wall. Select the words which best define the word *accuracy.*
   ☐ a. correctness or exactness
   ☐ b. size or height
   ☐ c. color or shade

2. Curran scowled at the wall, and spoke loudly with emphasis. The word *emphasis* means
   ☐ a. kindness.
   ☐ b. force.
   ☐ c. shame.

3. Miss Reed suggested that a blind man had been sent so that he wouldn't be able to identify Curran by sight. What does the word *identify* mean?
   ☐ a. recognize or point out
   ☐ b. strike or attack
   ☐ c. help or assist

4. "Never mind the alibi!" Mr. Curran snapped. Which of the following best defines the word *alibi*?
   ☐ a. time
   ☐ b. visitor
   ☐ c. excuse

☐ × 5 = ☐
NUMBER CORRECT   YOUR SCORE

☐ × 5 = ☐
NUMBER CORRECT   YOUR SCORE

IDENTIFYING STORY ELEMENTS. Each of the following questions tests your understanding of story elements. Put an *x* in the box next to each correct answer.

1. What is the *setting* of this story?
   ☐ a. a store
   ☐ b. a house
   ☐ c. an office

2. What happened last in the *plot* of the story?
   ☐ a. Henry Curran noticed that the clock on the wall said ten minutes to twelve.
   ☐ b. Miss Reed showed in an old man dressed completely in black.
   ☐ c. Curran said that he would see no visitors before four o'clock.

3. Identify the sentence which best *characterizes* Henry Curran.
   ☐ a. He was harsh and cruel.
   ☐ b. He was successful and kind.
   ☐ c. He played by civilized rules.

4. Which of the following statements best expresses the *theme* of "Appointment at Noon"?
   ☐ a. Not even the rich and powerful can cheat death.
   ☐ b. People should be more thoughtful to each other.
   ☐ c. Visitors can bring either good or bad news.

SELECTING WORDS FROM THE STORY. Complete the following paragraph by filling in each blank with one of the words listed below. Each of the words appears in the story. Since there are five words and four blanks, one word in the group will not be used.

When your watch or _____ says

twelve o'clock, that does not mean it is

lunchtime all over the country. In the United

States, there are _____ major time

zones. Moving from east to west, it is one

_____ earlier in each zone.

Therefore, if you are eating lunch at

_____ in New York City, your

friend in San Francisco may be eating

breakfast.

four   **clock**

door

hour   **noon**

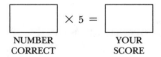

NUMBER   YOUR
CORRECT   SCORE

NUMBER   YOUR
CORRECT   SCORE

THINKING ABOUT THE STORY. Each of the following questions requires you to think critically about the selection. Put an *x* in the box next to the correct answer.

1. Henry Curran believed that jungle methods paid off. This suggests that Curran
   ☐ a. had many close business friends.
   ☐ b. was a very honest person.
   ☐ c. would do anything to achieve his goals.

2. Curran employed only those about whom he knew too much. Probably, Curran did this to
   ☐ a. make certain that his employees remained fearful and obedient.
   ☐ b. give work to people who would have trouble finding a job.
   ☐ c. prove that he was actually a very friendly person.

3. When the visitor looked at Curran, he was sorry, very sorry for what he saw. This suggests that Curran was a man to be
   ☐ a. admired.
   ☐ b. pitied.
   ☐ c. hated.

4. The visitor's appointment with Curran was at exactly two minutes to twelve. Why?
   ☐ a. That was the only time that Curran was willing to see him.
   ☐ b. That was the time when Curran was fated to die.
   ☐ c. That was the time when Miss Reed had made the appointment.

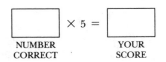

NUMBER CORRECT   × 5 =   YOUR SCORE

Thinking More About the Story

● How do you think Henry Curran's business acquaintances would have described him? Might some have admired Curran? Give reasons to support your point of view.
● Near the end of the story, Curran stood up and placed a thick, firm finger near the button on his desk. What do you think Curran was planning to do? What do you think would have happened then?
● Suppose that Curran had refused to see his visitor. Do you think that Death would have come for Curran at a different time? Explain.

Use the boxes below to total your scores for the exercises.

☐ **T**elling About the Story
+
☐ **W**atching for New Vocabulary Words
+
☐ **I**dentifying Story Elements
+
☐ **S**electing Words from the Story
+
☐ **T**hinking About the Story
▼
☐ **S**core Total: Story 14

15. Zoo

by Edward D. Hoch

*T*he children were always good during the month of August. This was especially so when it began to get near the twenty-third. For every year on the twenty-third of August, Professor Hugo's Interplanetary Zoo came to the Chicago area. The great silver spaceship would settle down in a huge parking area. It would remain there during its annual six-hour visit.

Long before daybreak large crowds would gather. Lines of children and adults, each one clutching his or her dollar, would wait restlessly to see the Professor's Interplanetary Zoo. Everyone was eager to see what race of strange creatures the Professor had brought this year.

In the past they had been treated to three-legged creatures from Venus. Or tall, thin men from Mars. Or snake-like horrors from some even more distant planet.

This year, as the large silver spaceship settled down to earth in the huge parking area just outside of Chicago, the children

95

watched with awe. They saw the sides of the spaceship slide up to reveal the usual cages made of thick bars. Inside the cages were some wild, small, horse-like animals that moved with quick, uneven motions and kept chattering in a high-pitched tone.

The citizens of Earth clustered around as Professor Hugo's crew quickly collected a dollar from everyone in the audience. Soon the good Professor, himself, made an appearance. He was wearing his many-colored cape and top hat.

"Peoples of Earth," he called into his microphone.

The crowd's noise died down and he continued. "Peoples of Earth," he went on, "this year we have a real treat for your dollar. Here are the little-known horse-spider people of Kaan—brought to you across a million miles of space at great expense. Gather around the amazing horse-spider people of Kaan. See them, study them, listen to them. Tell your friends about them. But hurry! My spaceship can remain here for only six hours!"

And the crowds slowly filed by, horrified and fascinated by these strange creatures that looked like horses, but ran up the walls of their cages like spiders. "This is certainly worth a dollar," one man remarked. "I'm going home to tell my wife."

All day long it went like that. Finally, ten thousand people had filed by the barred cages which were built into the side of the spaceship. Then, as the six-hour time limit ran out, Professor Hugo once more took the microphone in his hand.

"We must go now," said the Professor, "but we will return again next year on this date. And if you enjoyed Professor Hugo's Inter-

planetary Zoo this year, phone your friends in other cities. Tell them about it. We will land in New York tomorrow. Next week we go on to London, Paris, Rome, Hong Kong, and Tokyo. Then we must leave for other worlds!"

He waved farewell to them. And, as the ship rose from the ground, the Earth peoples agreed that this had been the very best Zoo yet. . . .

Two months and three planets later, the silver spaceship of Professor Hugo settled at last onto the familiar jagged rocks of Kaan. The horse-spider creatures filed quickly out of their cages. Professor Hugo was there to say a few parting words to them. Then the horse-spider creatures scurried away in a hundred different directions as they began seeking their homes among the rocks.

In one, the she-creature was happy to see the return of her mate and little one. She babbled a greeting in the strange Kaan language. Then she hurried to embrace them. "You were gone a long time," she said. "Was it good?"

The he-creature nodded. "Our little one enjoyed it especially," he said. "We visited eight worlds and saw many things."

The little one ran up the wall of the cave. "The place called Earth was the best. The creatures there wear garments over their skins, and they walk on two legs."

"But isn't it dangerous?" asked the she-creature.

"No," the he-creature answered. "There are bars to protect us from them. "We stay right in the ship. Next time you must come with us. It is well worth the nineteen commocs it costs."

The little one nodded. "It was the very best Zoo ever. . . ."

TELLING ABOUT THE STORY. Complete each of the following statements by putting an *x* in the box next to the correct answer. Each statement tells something about the story.

1. Every year, Professor Hugo's Interplanetary Zoo stayed in Chicago for
   ☐ a. six hours.
   ☐ b. two days.
   ☐ c. a month.

2. The Earth people agreed that Professor Hugo's latest zoo was
   ☐ a. not worth a dollar.
   ☐ b. not as good as earlier ones.
   ☐ c. the very best one yet.

3. The Earth people were fascinated by the creatures from Kaan because they
   ☐ a. spoke the same language as the Earth people.
   ☐ b. looked like horses and ran up the sides of their cages like spiders.
   ☐ c. were very tall and thin.

4. The little one from Kaan thought that the Earth people were unusual because they
   ☐ a. waited in long lines to see the Professor's Zoo.
   ☐ b. used dollars rather than commocs for money.
   ☐ c. wore garments and walked on two legs.

WATCHING FOR NEW VOCABULARY WORDS. Answer the following vocabulary questions by putting an *x* in the box next to the correct response.

1. Large crowds waited restlessly to see what race of strange creatures the Professor had brought. Which of the following best defines the word *restlessly*?
   ☐ a. unhappily
   ☐ b. impatiently
   ☐ c. thoughtlessly

2. The creatures of Kaan filed quickly out of their cages. As used in this sentence, the word *filed* means
   ☐ a. smoothed down with a metal tool.
   ☐ b. placed into a folder.
   ☐ c. walked in line.

3. As the large silver spaceship settled down, the children watched with awe. Define the word *awe*.
   ☐ a. wonder
   ☐ b. sorrow
   ☐ c. confidence

4. The she-creature, happy to see her mate and her little one, hurried to embrace them. What is the meaning of the word *embrace*?
   ☐ a. hug
   ☐ b. push
   ☐ c. locate

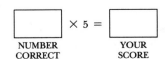

NUMBER CORRECT   × 5 =   YOUR SCORE

IDENTIFYING STORY ELEMENTS. Each of the following questions tests your understanding of story elements. Put an *x* in the box next to each correct answer.

1. When is "The Zoo" *set?*
   ☐ a. in the past
   ☐ b. in the present
   ☐ c. in the future

2. What happened first in the *plot* of the story?
   ☐ a. The Professor's spaceship returned to Kaan.
   ☐ b. Professor Hugo spoke to the citizens of Earth.
   ☐ c. The he-creature told his mate that he liked Earth the most.

3. Which sentence best *characterizes* Professor Hugo?
   ☐ a. He was famous for his magic tricks.
   ☐ b. He was a clever showman.
   ☐ c. He was an excellent teacher.

4. Which statement best describes the *theme* of the story?
   ☐ a. Sometimes, things which are only different, are considered strange.
   ☐ b. There are many different kinds of creatures in space.
   ☐ c. Zoos are fun to visit.

SELECTING WORDS FROM THE STORY. Complete the following paragraph by filling in each blank with one of the words listed below. Each of the words appears in the story. Since there are five words and four blanks, one word in the group will not be used.

Every year, _____ of people
                        1

visit the zoo in Washington, D.C. Many of

the visitors are young _____ who
                                  2

have come especially to see the Chinese

pandas which are housed there. These

_____ look very much like huge
         3

teddy bears. Every movement they make

amuses the large crowds which continually

_____ in front of their cage.
         4

time   children

gather

thousands   animals

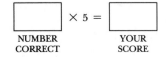

NUMBER   YOUR
CORRECT   SCORE

NUMBER   YOUR
CORRECT   SCORE

THINKING ABOUT THE STORY. Each of the following questions requires you to think critically about the selection. Put an *x* in the box next to the correct answer.

1. Probably, the children were very good just before the twenty-third of August because they
   ☐ a. enjoyed their summer vacation so much.
   ☐ b. wanted to be permitted to see the Professor's Zoo.
   ☐ c. had just visited Professor Hugo's Zoo.

2. Clues in the story suggest that Kaan is
   ☐ a. a world very near Earth.
   ☐ b. a planet very different from Earth.
   ☐ c. Professor Hugo's home.

3. We may infer that the Professor did not tell the creatures from Kaan that
   ☐ a. the trip would cost nineteen commocs.
   ☐ b. they would visit many strange worlds.
   ☐ c. the Earth peoples were paying to look at them.

4. This story suggests that things which are unfamiliar are
   ☐ a. viewed as fascinating and strange.
   ☐ b. not very interesting.
   ☐ c. not worth paying to look at.

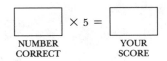

NUMBER CORRECT ☐ × 5 = ☐ YOUR SCORE

Thinking More About the Story

- What do you think Professor Hugo told the horse-spider creatures before they set off from Kaan on their journey through space? In your opinion, how good a business person was the Professor? Explain.
- The he-creature said that they visited eight worlds and saw many things. What do you think happened at each of the eight worlds they visited? (Describe the scene or scenes in as much detail as possible.)
- The statement, "Beauty is in the eye of the beholder," would apply very well to this story. Give reasons to support this statement.

Use the boxes below to total your scores for the exercises.

☐
+
Telling About the Story

☐
+
Watching for New Vocabulary Words

☐
+
Identifying Story Elements

☐
+
Selecting Words from the Story

☐
▼
Thinking About the Story

☐
Score Total: Story 15

99

16. A Trick of the Trade

by Dorothy S. Pratt

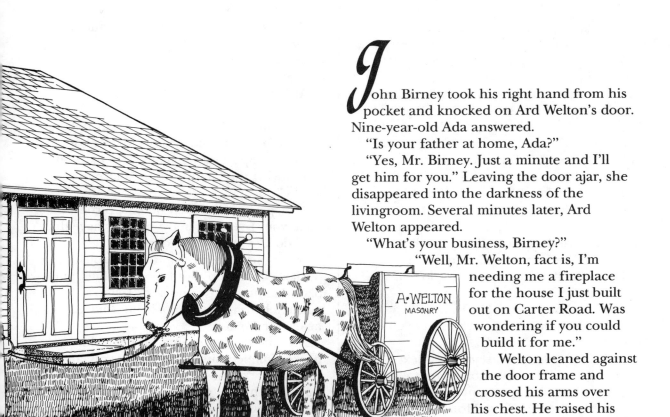

John Birney took his right hand from his pocket and knocked on Ard Welton's door. Nine-year-old Ada answered.

"Is your father at home, Ada?"

"Yes, Mr. Birney. Just a minute and I'll get him for you." Leaving the door ajar, she disappeared into the darkness of the livingroom. Several minutes later, Ard Welton appeared.

"What's your business, Birney?"

"Well, Mr. Welton, fact is, I'm needing me a fireplace for the house I just built out on Carter Road. Was wondering if you could build it for me."

Welton leaned against the door frame and crossed his arms over his chest. He raised his right hand to his chin and rubbed it thoughtfully.

"Being truthful, Birney, I've heard folks

101

say you're not too good about paying what you owe them. Now, I'm not going to spend my time building you a fireplace when I'm not going to get paid for it."

"Folks don't have no business talking that way about me. Why, what with Elsie and the five children, money just gets tight sometimes, that's all. I might pay a little bit slow now and then, but I always pay. Besides, it's getting near October and the nights are getting chilly already. My family needs that fireplace. And folks do say you're the best mason in Plymouth." He shoved his hands into his coat pockets and looked hopefully at Welton.

Welton looked back at him. His hand returned to his chin. Sure as he was born, Ard had heard from many a reputable man that Birney was real slow about paying his bills, when he bothered to pay them at all. And him with a good decent-paying job down at Seth Thomas! Folks said he squandered most of his pay, and they did work for Birney only for the sake of his children and Elsie, who was a decent enough type.

"Fact is, Birney, the job would cost you a hundred dollars. Now, I'll be needing half of that before I do the job, and the other half the day I'm finished. Won't do it any other way."

"Sounds good to me, Mr. Welton. I can come up with the money. When can you do the job?"

"Oh, I suppose I can start work next Monday, and I'll be over tomorrow to take a look at what you want done. Just remember—you be there Monday at seven in the morning with fifty dollars in your hand, or that fireplace won't get started."

"OK, Mr. Welton, sounds good. I'll be there

with the fifty dollars." He stuck out his right hand.

Welton took it briefly in his own. "OK, Birney. Good night now." He closed the door.

The following Monday morning, Ard drove his wagon up to the new Birney place at seven sharp. Sure enough, Birney was waiting for him, and walked up to the wagon as it came to a halt.

"Morning, Mr. Welton. Nice day."

"Morning, Birney. Got the money?"

"Well, Mr. Welton, fact is, I just couldn't get the whole fifty dollars up in so short a time. I've got forty dollars, though. Won't that be OK?"

Ard closed one eye and rubbed his chin. "Forty, eh?"

"I promise I'll have the other sixty dollars when you're finished! Please, Mr. Welton, it's awful important we get that fireplace in— I'm moving the family into the place in two weeks."

"Oh, give me the forty dollars, Birney. I'll build your fireplace, but you better have that sixty dollars the day I'm done."

Birney smiled and dug into his trouser pocket, coming up with four worn bills, and placed them one by one into Welton's outstretched hand. "I appreciate your good heart, Mr. Welton."

Ard put the money into his deep shirt pocket, jumped nimbly off the wagon, and went to work. Between that job and some surveying he was doing for the town, it took him nearly two weeks to finish. He sent word to Birney that he expected to see him on Monday morning at the new house.

He had laid the last stone and was

cleaning up when he saw Birney walking towards him. "Morning, Birney. Work's done."

"So I see. You do good work, Mr. Welton."

"That'll be sixty dollars."

Birney did not look at Ard. His eyes were glued to his brand-new chimney. "Well, Mr. Welton, fact is, I don't have it. Only worked a few days this week and . . ."

Ard didn't stay around to hear the rest. He picked up his tools, walked calmly to his wagon, climbed in, and drove away.

"Well," Birney said to himself, "that was a lot easier than I thought it would be. Welton's not as tough as everyone says he is." He laughed out loud at his own cleverness. "Nope. Welton think's he's a smart guy, but nobody gets one by old John Birney."

Two days later, he moved his family into the new house. After the furniture was in, he decided to light a fire in his new fireplace. He put a dry log in and lit the kindling. Slowly, it burst into flame.

"Looks good, don't it, Elsie? Hey, wait a minute—why's it so smoky in here? Smoke's not going up the chimney! Elsie, get me some water—got to put that fire out quick!" He did so, and ran outside to join his wife, coughing like a sick man. When the smoke had cleared a bit, he went back inside and opened the windows. "That Welton," he muttered to himself. "Thinks he's such a good mason."

An hour later, the room once again filled with fresh air, Birney went inside. He looked up the chimney and saw nothing but the sky. "I'm going over to South Street to see Welton," he told Elsie. "Who does he think he is, building me a fireplace that don't work?"

This time, when Birney knocked on his door, Ard opened it himself. He didn't look a bit surprised to see Birney standing there, and waited for him to speak.

"Your fireplace don't work."

"Don't work, eh?"

"That's right. I just lit it, and the smoke wouldn't go up the chimney. Why, Elsie and I nearly died."

"Look pretty healthy to me, Birney."

"Don't get smart with me, Welton. What's the matter with that fireplace?"

Ard stroked his chin and squinted at Birney. "Well, can't say that I know, Birney. I guess a man just can't expect much from a forty-dollar fireplace these days."

Birney opened his mouth but said nothing.

"You come up with sixty dollars, and I'll come down and take a look, but not a minute sooner."

"But Mr. Welton, we moved in today. We need that fireplace tonight. My poor little children are going to freeze to death!"

"Sixty dollars," said Ard, closing the door in Birney's face.

Two nights later, Birney once again knocked on the Welton door, and it was once again opened by Ard.

"I got your sixty dollars, Welton."

"Let's see it."

Birney dug the wad out of his pocket and slapped it into Ard's hand. Ard unrolled it and counted it. Twice.

"Yep, that's the sixty dollars you owe me all right." He started to close the door.

Birney put a hand up to keep it from closing. "Now wait a minute! When you coming over to fix my fireplace?"

"Your fireplace? Oh, that's right—you

claim your fireplace needs fixing. Well, can't make it tomorrow—I got a wedding and some surveying to do. I'll be over Sunday afternoon after dinner. Be there around two o'clock." He closed the door before Birney could answer.

Sunday afternoon at two-thirty, Welton drove up to the new Birney place. John Birney came outside to meet him.

"Afternoon, Birney. Family home?"

"Afternoon, Mr. Welton. Nope, they're all over at Elsie's folks having Sunday dinner."

Ard jumped off his wagon. He took out a ladder and a brick and walked to the house. Setting the ladder against the house, he quickly ascended to the roof, brick in hand. He walked up to the newly built chimney and looked down the shaft. Lifting the brick, he dropped it down the chimney, shattering the pane of glass he had mortared in so firmly the week before.

TELLING ABOUT THE STORY. Complete each of the following statements by putting an *x* in the box next to the correct answer. Each statement tells something about the story.

1. Ard Welton wasn't eager to build a fireplace for John Birney because Welton
   ☐ a. was too busy to find the time.
   ☐ b. had heard that Birney often didn't pay people what he owed them.
   ☐ c. didn't have the right tools and materials.

2. Welton agreed to build the fireplace if Birney paid him
   ☐ a. one hundred dollars before he began the job.
   ☐ b. sixty dollars before he began the job.
   ☐ c. fifty dollars before he began the job, and fifty dollars on the day he finished.

3. The first time Birney tried his new fireplace,
   ☐ a. it worked perfectly.
   ☐ b. smoke filled the room.
   ☐ c. there was no flame at all.

4. At the end of the story, Ard repaired the fireplace by
   ☐ a. building it over again.
   ☐ b. cementing in several more bricks.
   ☐ c. breaking the piece of glass that was blocking the chimney.

WATCHING FOR NEW VOCABULARY WORDS. Answer the following vocabulary questions by putting an *x* in the box next to the correct response.

1. Leaving the door ajar, Ada disappeared into the darkness of the living room. The word *ajar* means
   ☐ a. slightly open.
   ☐ b. broken.
   ☐ c. shaking.

2. Folks said that Birney squandered most of his pay. Define the word *squandered*.
   ☐ a. lost
   ☐ b. earned
   ☐ c. wasted

3. After he set the ladder against the house, Ard ascended to the roof. The word *ascended* means
   ☐ a. went up or climbed.
   ☐ b. fell down or tripped.
   ☐ c. stared or looked hard.

4. Birney wanted Ard to build his fireplace because Ard was considered the best mason in town. A *mason* is a person who
   ☐ a. works with wood and paint.
   ☐ b. works with stone and bricks.
   ☐ c. makes a living repairing cars.

[ ] × 5 = [ ]

NUMBER CORRECT   YOUR SCORE

[ ] × 5 = [ ]

NUMBER CORRECT   YOUR SCORE

IDENTIFYING STORY ELEMENTS. Each of the following questions tests your understanding of story elements. Put an *x* in the box next to each correct answer.

1. "A Trick of the Trade" is *set*
   ☐ a. in a small town.
   ☐ b. in a very large city.
   ☐ c. on a farm.

2. What happened last in the *plot* of the story?
   ☐ a. John Birney moved his family into the new house.
   ☐ b. Birney complained to Ard that the fireplace didn't work.
   ☐ c. Birney knocked on the Weltons' door and gave Ard sixty dollars.

3. Which one of the following sentences best *characterizes* John Birney?
   ☐ a. He was very slow about paying his bills, when he paid them at all.
   ☐ b. He was out of work, and therefore couldn't pay his bills.
   ☐ c. He had a reputation for being very honest.

4. Identify the sentence which best expresses the *theme* of the story.
   ☐ a. Some families use fireplaces to heat their homes.
   ☐ b. A cheater finds himself tricked.
   ☐ c. It is very hard to find workers who do a good job.

☐ × 5 = ☐
NUMBER CORRECT   YOUR SCORE

SELECTING WORDS FROM THE STORY. Complete the following paragraph by filling in each blank with one of the words listed below. Each of the words appears in the story. Since there are five words and four blanks, one word in the group will not be used.

Nothing beats a roaring fire on a damp and _____ winter's night. I can
                    1
_____ hours staring at a burning
         2
_____ as I watch the flames leap
         3
up and down. There are few things that are more relaxing. Have you ever tried popping corn in a fireplace? It's tricky and you've got to be careful, but it sure tastes

_____ .
         4

spend   important

log

good   chilly

☐ × 5 = ☐
NUMBER CORRECT   YOUR SCORE

106

THINKING ABOUT THE STORY. Each of the following questions requires you to think critically about the selection. Put an *x* in the box next to the correct answer.

1. When John Birney came to Ard Welton's house and complained about the fireplace, Ard was probably
   ☐ a. very surprised to see him.
   ☐ b. not surprised to see him.
   ☐ c. afraid that Birney would take him to court.

2. Evidence in the story indicates that Ard suspected that Birney would
   ☐ a. try to get away without paying the balance on his bill.
   ☐ b. pay the rest of the money on the day the fireplace was finished.
   ☐ c. hire someone else to have the fireplace repaired.

3. Birney didn't realize that the chimney was blocked because he
   ☐ a. didn't look up the chimney.
   ☐ b. had never seen a blocked chimney before.
   ☐ c. couldn't see the glass when he looked up the chimney.

4. We may infer that Ard Welton was
   ☐ a. inexperienced at building fireplaces.
   ☐ b. very experienced at building fireplaces.
   ☐ c. a good worker, but was not too clever.

$$\boxed{} \times 5 = \boxed{}$$

NUMBER CORRECT   YOUR SCORE

Thinking More About the Story

- Why is this story called "A Trick of the Trade"? Do you think it is a good title? Explain.
- When Birney at first refused to pay the sixty dollars, Ard picked up his tools and calmly drove away. Why wasn't Ard upset or worried? Why did Birney think that Ard was not "as tough as everyone says he is"? Did this prove to be the case? Give reasons to support your answers.
- Suppose a neighbor asked Birney to recommend someone to build a fireplace. Do you think Birney would suggest Ard Welton? Explain your answer.

Use the boxes below to total your scores for the exercises.

☐ **T**elling About the Story
+
☐ **W**atching for New Vocabulary Words
+
☐ **I**dentifying Story Elements
+
☐ **S**electing Words from the Story
+
☐ **T**hinking About the Story
▼
☐ **S**core Total: Story 16

17. Underwater Test

by Robert Zacks

Jimmy stood at attention on the deck of the new submarine with the rest of the crew. At that moment, he felt both pride and a strange unhappiness.

Going to special submarine school had been tough, but he'd finally made it. He was proud to be a member of an outstanding group where every person was handpicked and a volunteer. This was something Jimmy had hungered for. He liked the idea of being part of a tightly knit group of friends who worked closely together on a dangerous and complicated job.

But something had gone wrong. Somehow, he didn't seem to belong. *Don't they like me?* he wondered in misery, as he stared out at the dock. *Is that it? Don't they like me?*

Everything else matched his dream.

The new submarine tugged at the dock mooring, as if eager to slide into the vast ocean depths. It swelled Jimmy's lungs with pleasure. But what good was it if they didn't like him? Commander Philips had greeted him coldly. The crew members were also very distant. They seemed to be coated with an invisible varnish that kept Jimmy's smiles sliding off, leaving them untouched.

It left Jimmy with a frightened feeling, a strange feeling of dismay that kept his nerves on edge. He listened now, unhappily, as Commander Philips addressed the group. His words were sharp in the clear, cold air.

"This is a brand new sub," said Commander Philips. "We're going to check it out on a shakedown cruise." He paused and then continued a bit grimly. "As you know, a sub isn't like other ships. Something can go wrong on a surface ship and it won't matter too much. A sub, however, is *under* water—so it can matter very much. All the equipment on this new sub has been tested and re-tested, of course, but not on an actual underwater run. So it can be a tricky business, this first cruise."

Commander Philips ran his eyes over the faces of the crew. "You're all experienced men, except one of you who is new. However, he has been trained. On *shore* school," added the Commander.

The men grinned, and Jimmy flushed. "All right," the Commander said crisply, "Down you go, men. Take your diving stations!"

The men broke their ranks and climbed smoothly down the ladder and into the sub. When Jimmy descended, he felt tense and awkward. He almost slipped on a rung. It shook him up to have that happen on his first dive. He felt alone and apart from the others. He became aware that a couple of men were watching him from the corners of their eyes as they hurried past him to their stations.

Larry Parker was the Electrician's Mate. He followed Jimmy through the narrow passage past the small radio shack to the Control Room. As Jimmy took his station, he became aware that Larry was staring at him.

"Look, Jimmy boy," said Larry, finally, "don't worry about the *dive*. It's coming *up* that's the problem."

"You do your job," said Jimmy in quiet anger. "I'll do mine."

He didn't like Larry, who had been the unfriendliest of them all. He felt that Larry mocked him with jeering advice. Larry shrugged his shoulders and said sharply, "Okay. Just be on your toes, sonny. This is no kindergarten you picked to come into. One mistake and we could all be dead. The biggest worry is fire which could . . ."

"I know all that," Jimmy interrupted angrily.

"You're a pretty fresh kid," said Larry. "I got a feeling we're not going to get along."

"That goes for me, too," said Jimmy bitterly.

They glared at each other. As Larry turned coldly away, Jimmy was filled with misery. Oh, this was just fine, wasn't it, just dandy, arguing this way. What would it be like on long, lonely cruises underwater for weeks at a time with all that crew hating him?

There was a lump in Jimmy's throat as he watched Larry turn away with scorn to his own station. Where, thought Jimmy, was that great bond of friendship submariners were so famous for? He wanted to be part of this crew because only the best applicants could get in. Jimmy remembered the tests he'd been given. He'd come through every one with flying colors.

But, he thought in dismay, *these guys must sense how scared I am. That must be it. That's it!*

For he was indeed frightened—frightened to death of going under water. All his instincts as a sailor had been to stay on the *surface* where there was air. *Under* water brought visions of a ship sunk and broken, and of men drowning, gasping for air, choking, with lungs filled with strangling, thick water. Despite himself, Jimmy shivered.

Commander Philips came down the ladder and suddenly there was a tension, an alertness. Men stared at dials intently. Orders were given in crisp, prompt tones. Levers were pulled, buttons pushed. There was the sound of faintly humming motors and a sense of motion. Then the floor tilted slightly, and after a while the sub levelled off and rolled a bit, like a huge log going under water.

Jimmy drew in a deep breath and filled his lungs. This wasn't bad, not bad at all. He found himself grinning around in delight and saw Commander Philips nod to Larry, then walk toward the After Battery Compartment. The air was becoming stale and musty.

Then Jimmy noticed the strained look on Larry's face. Larry twitched his nostrils and looked up alertly. "Smell anything?" he said sharply to the other men in the control room.

"No," said one of them after taking a deep breath.

"I do," said Larry, stubbornly. He quickly spoke into the communicator. "Commander Philips. Commander Philips." Larry nervously swung his gaze around. "Hey, *it's dead.* Something's going wrong! Get the Commander! You, Jerry, get to the radio shack. See if the sending equipment's okay."

Jimmy's heart seemed to become a solid sickening weight. Then it sprang into terrified life. He'd never seen men move so fast before. They could *feel* when something was wrong—the way a musician knows when one small wrong note has been hit by a player in an orchestra.

"What is it?" Jimmy asked, keeping his voice steady. Suddenly, he was aware of the huge weight of water pressing hungrily on the submarine. Panic rose in him. "Hey, what . . ."

"Keep an eye on your instruments!" Larry snapped.

Jimmy turned. He heard a gurgling, then a splashing. A yell came from his throat as a solid stream of rushing water swirled around his ankles. Wildly he turned and saw the water coming in swiftly through a widening hole.

"Main intake valve open!" screamed Jimmy immediately. In a flash Jimmy knew that in minutes the sub could take in enough water to flood the ship. The main intake valve was thirty-one inches in diameter. At that moment the communicator returned to life. Larry grabbed it.

Larry yelled into it, "Main intake valve open! The main intake valve is open!"

Commander Philips' voice immediately came back, steady and controlled. With horror Jimmy heard what he ordered. The Commander's words were directed at some unseen sailor in the After Battery Compartment which was next to the Control Room. "Close watertight doors!" ordered the Commander. "Shut off Control Room!"

It was a death warrant! Jimmy stood there, shocked. The water was up to his knees now, rising rapidly. They were swinging closed the heavy door. They were shutting him and the flooding area off fast to save the sub and the men in the other compartments. If they didn't do it, they *all* would die.

"Larry," yelled Jimmy. "We better get out of here!"

Larry turned a strained face toward him. "No. Come here, quickly. We've got to get the main intake valve closed. We might be able to do it. Hurry."

The watertight doors were closing.

The freezing water was up to Jimmy's waist. He wanted to scream and run. There were only minutes between him and a horrible death. Nobody would ever know. He could leave Larry and save himself! He could . . .

"All right," Jimmy groaned. He reached through the sweeping water toward the main intake valve. He seized a control wheel and desperately tried to turn it shut. To his amazement it slowly closed. The torrent of water became a trickle. "Look," he yelled. "It's closing. It . . ."

He stopped.

Larry was grinning at him. From behind him, Commander Philips and the other men came sloshing in the waist-high water through the watertight doors which had opened again. They had big smiles on their faces.

"Okay," said Commander Philips briskly. "Up and out on deck, everybody."

"But . . . but we're under water," said Jimmy, dazed. "I don't . . ."

He stopped and gulped as Larry, who'd climbed the ladder, opened the tower. Light streamed down from the opening—bright glorious daylight.

"We never left the dock," said Commander Philips. "We've been on the surface all along. This isn't a real seagoing sub you're on, son. It's a special training job."

"What a rotten trick!" shouted Jimmy.

"It was no trick," said Commander Philips quietly. "It's the last test you had to take. We had to see how you'd act in a life-and-death emergency. We had to see if you'd break."

The Commander looked around at the crew with pleasure in his eyes. "Every man here passed the same test. It wasn't easy for them to be unfriendly to you, but they were acting under orders. We wanted to give you every reason to turn and run." The Commander paused, smiling. "But you didn't. You're one of us now, Jimmy. We know we can depend on you."

Jimmy looked at the friendly faces, at the cheerful grins. He knew then that he had found his shipmates.

TELLING ABOUT THE STORY. Complete each of the following statements by putting an *x* in the box next to the correct answer. Each statement tells something about the story.

1. At the beginning of the story, Jimmy was unhappy because he
   - ☐ a. thought that the other men didn't like him.
   - ☐ b. hadn't done well on his tests.
   - ☐ c. was lonely for home.

2. Water was pouring into the ship because
   - ☐ a. there was a large hole in the submarine.
   - ☐ b. a fire had damaged one of the compartments.
   - ☐ c. the main intake valve was open.

3. The Commander ordered a sailor to
   - ☐ a. radio for help.
   - ☐ b. abandon the ship.
   - ☐ c. shut off the Control Room.

4. At the end of the story, Jimmy learned that
   - ☐ a. he had saved the ship from sinking.
   - ☐ b. the ship had been on the surface all along.
   - ☐ c. he could not depend upon the other men for help.

WATCHING FOR NEW VOCABULARY WORDS. Answer the following vocabulary questions by putting an *x* in the box next to the correct response.

1. Jimmy liked the idea of working on a dangerous and complicated job. Which of the following best defines the word *complicated?*
   - ☐ a. simple
   - ☐ b. difficult
   - ☐ c. lonely

2. Larry thought that he smelled something because the air was becoming stale and musty. The word *musty* means
   - ☐ a. pure or fresh.
   - ☐ b. damp or moldy.
   - ☐ c. slow or delayed.

3. Where, Jimmy wondered, was the great bond of friendship submariners were famous for? As used in this sentence, the word *bond* means
   - ☐ a. link.
   - ☐ b. sum of money.
   - ☐ c. certificate.

4. After the intake valve was shut, the torrent of water became a trickle. What is the meaning of the word *torrent?*
   - ☐ a. flood
   - ☐ b. dripping
   - ☐ c. group

<table>
<tr><td>☐</td><td>× 5 =</td><td>☐</td></tr>
<tr><td>NUMBER CORRECT</td><td></td><td>YOUR SCORE</td></tr>
</table>

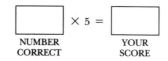

<table>
<tr><td>☐</td><td>× 5 =</td><td>☐</td></tr>
<tr><td>NUMBER CORRECT</td><td></td><td>YOUR SCORE</td></tr>
</table>

IDENTIFYING STORY ELEMENTS. Each of the following questions tests your understanding of story elements. Put an *x* in the box next to each correct answer.

1. Where is "Underwater Test" *set?*
   ☐ a. on a dock
   ☐ b. at a special submarine school
   ☐ c. on a submarine

2. What happened last in the *plot* of the story?
   ☐ a. Larry and Jimmy glared at each other, and exchanged harsh words.
   ☐ b. Jimmy seized a control valve and began to turn it shut.
   ☐ c. A stream of water swirled around Jimmy's ankles.

3. Which of the following sentences best *characterizes* Jimmy?
   ☐ a. He didn't enjoy working closely with others.
   ☐ b. He was pleased to be a member of the crew, but he felt like an outsider.
   ☐ c. He was too scared to do his job properly.

4. Identify the statement which best expresses the *theme* of the story.
   ☐ a. To finally be accepted, a newcomer must pass a difficult test.
   ☐ b. Life on a submarine is sometimes very dangerous.
   ☐ c. Many people are very frightened of going under water.

☐ × 5 = ☐
NUMBER CORRECT   YOUR SCORE

SELECTING WORDS FROM THE STORY. Complete the following paragraph by filling in each blank with one of the words listed below. Each of the words appears in the story. Since there are five words and four blanks, one word in the group will not be used.

Life aboard a submarine is often difficult and is sometimes very _____ . Once the craft drops beneath the _____ , it may remain underwater for days, weeks, or even months. Space and activities are limited. However there is one special advantage to being a member of a submarine _____ . Some of the _____ food in the Navy is served on submarines.

crew   throat

surface

best   dangerous

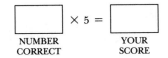

NUMBER CORRECT   YOUR SCORE

113

THINKING ABOUT THE STORY. Each of the following questions requires you to think critically about the selection. Put an *x* in the box next to the correct answer.

1. We may infer that Larry
   ☐ a. hated Jimmy.
   ☐ b. pretended not to like Jimmy.
   ☐ c. was not a very good sailor.

2. Which one of the following statements is true?
   ☐ a. The submarine was deep under water.
   ☐ b. The submarine was never really in danger of sinking.
   ☐ c. The submarine was a real sea-going sub.

3. The main purpose of the test was to determine if the new sailor
   ☐ a. was intelligent.
   ☐ b. was strong.
   ☐ c. could be trusted.

4. The last paragraph of the story suggests that the crew members
   ☐ a. will continue to be unfriendly to Jimmy.
   ☐ b. will act differently to Jimmy now.
   ☐ c. were sorry that Jimmy passed the test.

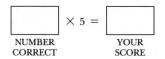

☐ × 5 = ☐

NUMBER CORRECT   YOUR SCORE

Thinking More About the Story

- Jimmy saw Commander Philips nod to Larry, then walk to the After Battery Compartment. The air then became stale and musty. What do you suspect happened during those few moments? Explain.
- Why were the crew members instructed to be unfriendly to Jimmy? Couldn't the same goal have been achieved if they had been very friendly to him? Explain why the story is called "Underwater Test."
- Suppose Jimmy had rushed out of the compartment to save himself from the rising water. How do you think the story would have ended?

Use the boxes below to total your scores for the exercises.

☐
   +
Telling About the Story

☐
   +
Watching for New Vocabulary Words

☐
   +
Identifying Story Elements

☐
   +
Selecting Words from the Story

☐
   ▼
Thinking About the Story

☐
Score Total: Story 17

18. The Right Kind of House

by Henry Slesar

The automobile that stopped in front of Aaron Hacker's real-estate office had a New York license plate. Aaron didn't need to see the license plate to know that its owner was new to the elm-shaded town of Ivy Corners. The car was a red convertible. There was nothing else like it in town.

The man got out of the car and headed straight for the door.

"It seems to be a customer," said Mr. Hacker to the young lady at the other desk "Let's look busy."

It was a customer, all right. The man had a folded newspaper in his right hand. He was a bit on the heavy side and wore a light gray suit. He was about fifty with dark, curly hair. The skin of his face was flushed and hot, but his narrow eyes were frosty-clear. He came through the doorway and nodded at Aaron. "Are you Mr. Hacker?"

"Yes, sir," Aaron smiled. "What can I do for you?"

The man waved the newspaper. "I saw the name of your agency in the real-estate section of the newspaper."

"Yep. I take an ad every week. Lots of city people are interested in a town like ours, Mr—"

"Waterbury," the man said. He pulled a white handkerchief out of his pocket and mopped his face. "Hot today."

"Unusually hot," Aaron answered. "Doesn't often get so hot in our town. We're near the lake, you know. Well. Won't you sit down, Mr. Waterbury?"

"Thank you." The man took the chair, and sighed. "I've been driving around. Thought I'd look the town over before I came here. Very nice little place."

"Yes, we like it," said Aaron.

"Now I really don't have much time, Mr. Hacker. Suppose we get right down to business."

"Suits me, Mr. Waterbury. Well, then, was there any place in particular you were interested in?"

"As a matter of fact, yes. I saw a house at the edge of town, across the way from an old deserted building."

"Was it an old yellow house with pillars?" asked Aaron.

"Yes. That's the place. I thought I saw a 'For Sale' sign, but I wasn't sure. Do you have that house listed?"

Aaron chuckled softly. "Yep, we got it listed all right." He flipped through a loose-leaf book, and pointed to a typewritten sheet. "But you won't be interested for long."

"Why not?"

Aaron turned the book around. "Read it for yourself."

The man did so:

> AUTHENTIC COLONIAL: Eight rooms, two baths, large porches, trees and shrubbery. Near shopping and schools. $75,000.

"Still interested?"

The man stirred uncomfortably. "Why not? Something wrong with it?"

"Well." Aaron scratched his temple. "If you really like this town, Mr. Waterbury— I mean if you really want to settle here, I have any number of places that'd suit you better."

"Now, just a minute!" The man looked indignant. I'm asking you about *this* colonial house. You want to sell it or not?"

"Do I?" Aaron chuckled. "Mister, I've had that property on my hands for five years. There's no house I'd rather collect a commission on. Only my luck ain't that good."

"What do you mean?"

"I mean you won't buy. That's what I mean. I keep the listing on my books just for the sake of old Sadie Grimes. Otherwise, I wouldn't waste the space. Believe me."

"I don't get you."

"Then let me explain. Mrs. Grimes put her place up for sale five years ago, when her son died. She gave me the job of selling it. I didn't want the job—no sir! I told her that to her face. I mean the old place ain't even worth $10,000!"

The man swallowed. "Ten? And she wants $75,000?"

"That's right. It's a real old house. I mean *old.* Some of the beams will be going in the next couple of years. Basement's full of water half the time. Upper floor leans to the right about nine inches. And the grounds are a mess."

"Then why does she ask so much?"

Aaron shrugged. "Don't ask me. Sentiment, maybe. The house has been in her family since the Revolution. Something like that."

The man looked at the floor. "That's too bad," he said. "Too bad!" He looked up at Aaron and smiled sheepishly. "And I kinda liked the place. It was—I don't know how to explain it—the *right* kind of house."

"I know what you mean. It's a friendly old place. A good buy at $10,000. But $75,000?" He laughed. "I think I know Sadie's reasoning, though. You see, she doesn't have much money. Her son was supporting her, doing well in the city. Then he died, and she knew that it was sensible to sell. But she couldn't bring herself to part with the old place. So she set a price tag so high that *nobody* would buy it. That eased her conscience." Mr. Hacker shook his head sadly. "It's a strange world, ain't it?"

"Yes," Waterbury said thoughtfully.

"Then he stood up. "Tell you what, Mr. Hacker. Suppose I drive out to see Mrs. Grimes? Suppose I talk to her about it, get her to change her price."

"You're fooling yourself, Mr. Waterbury. I've been trying for five years."

"Who knows? Maybe if somebody *else* tried—"

Aaron Hacker shrugged his shoulders. "Who knows, is right. It's a strange world, Mr. Waterbury. If you're willing to go to the trouble, I'll be only too happy to lend a hand."

"Good. Then I'll leave now . . ."

"Fine! You just let me ring Sadie Grimes. I'll tell her you're on your way."

Waterbury drove slowly through the quiet streets. The trees that lined the avenues cast peaceful shadows on the hood of the car.

He reached the home of Sadie Grimes without once passing another moving vehicle. He parked his car beside the rotted picket fence that faced the house.

The lawn was a jungle of weeds and crabgrass, and the columns that rose from the front porch were covered with flaking paint.

There was a hand knocker on the door. He banged it twice.

The woman who came to the door was short and plump. Her hair was white and her face was lined. She wore a heavy wool sweater, despite the heat.

"You must be Mr. Waterbury," she said. "Aaron Hacker said you were coming."

"Yes." The man smiled. "How do you do, Mrs. Grimes?"

"About as well as I can expect. I suppose you want to come in?"

"It's awfully hot out here." He chuckled.

"Hm. Well, come in then. I've put some lemonade in the ice-box. Only don't expect me to bargain with you, Mr. Waterbury. I'm not that kind of person."

"Of course not," the man said, and followed her inside.

They entered a square parlor with heavy furniture. The only color in the room was in the faded hues of the worn rug in the center of the bare floor.

The old woman headed straight for a rocker, and sat motionless, her wrinkled hands folded sternly.

"Well?" she said. "If you have anything to say, Mr. Waterbury, I suggest you say it."

The man cleared his throat. "Mrs. Grimes, I've just spoken with your real-estate agent—"

"I know all that," she snapped. "Aaron's a fool. All the more for letting you come here with the notion of changing my mind. I'm too old for changing my mind, Mr. Waterbury."

"Er—well, I don't know if that was my intention, Mrs. Grimes. I thought we'd just—talk a little."

She leaned back, and the rocker squeaked. "Talk's free. Say what you like."

"Yes." He mopped his face again, and shoved the handkerchief back into his pocket. "Well, let me put it this way, Mrs. Grimes. I'm a business man—a bachelor—never married, I live alone. I've worked for a long time, and I've made a fair amount of money. Now I'm ready to retire—to somewhere quiet. I like Ivy Corners. I passed through here some years ago on my way to—er, Albany. I thought one day I might like to settle here."

"So?"

"So, when I drove through your town today, and saw this house, it just seemed—right for me."

"I like it too, Mr. Waterbury. That's why I'm asking a fair price for it."

Waterbury blinked. "Fair price? You'll have to admit, Mrs. Grimes, these days a house like this shouldn't cost more than—"

"That's enough!" the woman cried. "I told you, Mr. Waterbury, I don't want to sit here all day and argue with you. If you won't pay my price, then we can forget all about it."

"But, Mrs. Grimes—"

"Good *day,* Mr. Waterbury!"

She stood up, indicating that he was expected to leave.

But he didn't. "Wait a minute, Mrs. Grimes," he said. "Just a moment. I know it's crazy, but—all right. I'll pay what you want."

She looked at him for a long moment. "Are you sure, Mr. Waterbury?"

"Positive! I've enough money. If that's the only way you'll have it, that's the way it'll be."

She smiled. "I think that lemonade'll be cold enough. I'll bring you some—and then I'll tell you something about this house."

He was mopping his brow when she returned with the tray. He gulped at the frosty yellow beverage greedily.

"This house," she said, easing back in her rocker, "has been in my family since 1802. It was built fifteen years before that. Every member of the family, except my son, Michael, was born in the bedroom upstairs.

"I know it's not the most solid house in Ivy Corners. After Michael was born, there was a flood in the basement, and we never seemed to get it dry since. I love the old place, though, you understand."

"Of course," Waterbury said.

"Michael's father died when Michael was nine. There were hard times then. I did some needlework, and my own father had left me some money which supports me today. Not in very grand style, but I manage. Michael missed his father, perhaps even more than I. He grew up to be, well, wild is the only word that comes to mind."

The man nodded with understanding.

"When he graduated from high school, Michael left Ivy Corners and went to the city. He went there against my wishes, make no mistake. But he was like so many young men—full of ambition, wild ambition. I didn't know what he did in the city. But he must have been successful—he sent me money regularly. However, I didn't see him for nine years."

"Ah," the man sighed, sadly.

"Yes, it wasn't easy for me. But it was even worse when Michael came home. Because, when he did, he was in trouble."

"Oh?"

"I didn't know how bad the trouble was. He showed up in the middle of the night, looking thinner and older than I could have believed possible. He had no luggage with him, only a small black suitcase. When I tried to take it from him, he almost struck me. Struck *me*—his own mother!

"I put him to bed myself, as if he was a little boy again. I could hear him crying out during the night.

"The next day, he told me to leave the house. Just for a few hours. He wanted to do something, he said. He didn't explain what. But when I returned that evening, I noticed that the little black suitcase was gone."

The man's eyes widened over the lemonade glass.

"What did it mean?" he asked.

"I didn't know then. But I found out soon—too terribly soon. That night, a man came to our house. I don't even know how he got in. I first knew when I heard voices in Michael's room. I went to the door, and tried to listen, tried to find out what sort of trouble my boy was in. But I heard only shouts and threats, and then . . ."

She paused, and her shoulders sagged.

"And a shot," she continued, "a gunshot. When I went into the room, I found the bedroom window open, and the stranger gone. And Michael—he was on the floor. He was dead!"

The chair creaked.

"That was five years ago," she said. "Five long years. It was a while before I realized what had happened. The police told me the story. Michael and this other man had been involved in a crime, a serious crime. They had stolen many, many thousands of dollars.

"Michael had taken that money, and run off with it. He wanted to keep it all for himself. He hid it somewhere in this house—to this very day I don't know where. The other man had come looking for my son, looking to collect his share. When he found the money gone, he—he killed my boy."

She looked up. "That's when I put this house up for sale—at $75,000. I knew that, someday, my son's killer would return to look for the money. Someday, he would want this house at any price. All I had to do was wait until I found the man willing to pay much too much for an old lady's house."

She rocked gently in the chair.

Waterbury put down the empty glass and licked his lips. He was having trouble keeping his eyes open, and his head was growing very, very dizzy.

"*Ugh!*" he said. "This lemonade is bitter."

TELLING ABOUT THE STORY. Complete each of the following statements by putting an *x* in the box next to the correct answer. Each statement tells something about the story.

1. Mr. Waterbury came to Ivy Corners to
   - ☐ a. retire.
   - ☐ b. buy an old house.
   - ☐ c. go into the real estate business.

2. According to Aaron Hacker, Mrs. Grimes' house was
   - ☐ a. very beautiful.
   - ☐ b. worth $75,000.
   - ☐ c. in very bad condition.

3. Mr. Grimes' son, Michael, was
   - ☐ a. never in trouble.
   - ☐ b. usually out of money.
   - ☐ c. shot by another man.

4. At the end of the story, we learn that Mrs. Grimes was looking for
   - ☐ a. someone to fix up her house.
   - ☐ b. money that had been hidden in the basement.
   - ☐ c. the man who killed her son.

WATCHING FOR NEW VOCABULARY WORDS. Answer the following vocabulary questions by putting an *x* in the box next to the correct response.

1. Mrs. Grimes' house was listed as an "authentic colonial." The word *authentic* means
   - ☐ a. real.
   - ☐ b. false.
   - ☐ c. broken.

2. Aaron Hacker suggested that Mrs. Grimes didn't want to sell the house because of sentiment—it had been in her family since the Revolution. Which phrase best defines the word *sentiment?*
   - ☐ a. strong feelings
   - ☐ b. lack of concern
   - ☐ c. great wealth

3. Aaron Hacker thought for a moment, then scratched his temple. As used in this sentence, the word *temple* means
   - ☐ a. a place to worship.
   - ☐ b. the side of the forehead.
   - ☐ c. a looseleaf notebook.

4. The only color in the room was in the faded hues of the worn rug. What is the meaning of the word *hues?*
   - ☐ a. shades or tints
   - ☐ b. cotton or wool
   - ☐ c. earth or mud

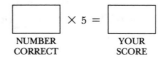

NUMBER CORRECT   × 5 =   YOUR SCORE

NUMBER CORRECT   × 5 =   YOUR SCORE

IDENTIFYING STORY ELEMENTS. Each of the following questions tests your understanding of story elements. Put an *x* in the box next to each correct answer.

1. What happened last in the *plot* of the story?
   - ☐ a. Mr. Waterbury said that he saw a house he liked at the edge of town.
   - ☐ b. Mr. Waterbury was having trouble keeping his eyes open.
   - ☐ c. Mrs. Grimes brought Waterbury some lemonade on a tray.

2. Which sentence best *characterizes* Mrs. Grimes?
   - ☐ a. She was the kind of person who could easily be persuaded to change her mind.
   - ☐ b. When she set her mind on something, she was patient and determined.
   - ☐ c. She always approved of the actions of her child.

3. Select the word which best describes the *mood* of the story.
   - ☐ a. cheerful
   - ☐ b. serious
   - ☐ c. humorous

4. The *theme* of this story deals with
   - ☐ a. friendship.
   - ☐ b. power.
   - ☐ c. revenge.

	× 5 =	
NUMBER CORRECT		YOUR SCORE

SELECTING WORDS FROM THE STORY. Complete the following paragraph by filling in each blank with one of the words listed below. Each of the words appears in the story. Since there are five words and four blanks, one word in the group will not be used.

There is no *one* kind of house which is right for everyone. The first Eskimos who _____ (1) in freezing Alaska built igloos made of blocks of ice. People who live in very warm areas build houses to _____ (2) the hot climate. Their homes often have open, outdoor _____ (3) called patios or courtyards. People who live at the _____ (4) of a river or lake sometimes build their houses high above ground to prevent flooding from rising water.

jungle   **suit**

settled

edge   **spaces**

	× 5 =	
NUMBER CORRECT		YOUR SCORE

121

THINKING ABOUT THE STORY. Each of the following questions requires you to think critically about the selection. Put an *x* in the box next to the correct answer.

1. We may infer that five years ago, Mr. Waterbury
   ☐ a. murdered Michael Grimes.
   ☐ b. passed Ivy Corners on his way to Albany.
   ☐ c. met Michael Grimes for the first time.

2. Evidence in the story indicates that Mrs. Grimes
   ☐ a. was really very rich.
   ☐ b. would eventually have sold her house for less money.
   ☐ c. poisoned Mr. Waterbury.

3. Probably, Mr. Waterbury wanted to buy the house in order to
   ☐ a. make Mrs. Grimes happy.
   ☐ b. search it for a suitcase filled with money.
   ☐ c. sell it later for a higher price.

4. Mrs. Grimes set an extremely high price for her house because she
   ☐ a. thought it was worth the money.
   ☐ b. knew that only her son's killer would be willing to pay it.
   ☐ c. didn't want anyone to inquire about it.

	× 5 =	
NUMBER CORRECT		YOUR SCORE

Thinking More About the Story

- Mr. Waterbury said that he came to like the town of Ivy Corners when he first passed through it some years ago on his way to Albany. Was Mr. Waterbury telling the truth? Why did he tell Mrs. Grimes this story?
- Mrs. Grimes didn't offer Mr. Waterbury a glass of lemonade until he agreed to buy the house. Why? Suppose Waterbury had refused to pay $75,000 for the house. What do you think would have happened then?
- Why didn't Mrs. Grimes tell Aaron Hacker the real reason she was asking so much money for her house? Do you think Mr. Hacker would have been willing to go along with her plan? What might he have done? Explain.

Use the boxes below to total your scores for the exercises.

+	**T**elling About the Story
+	**W**atching for New Vocabulary Words
+	**I**dentifying Story Elements
+	**S**electing Words from the Story
▼	**T**hinking About the Story
	Score Total: Story 18

Acknowledgments

Acknowledgment is gratefully made to the following publishers, authors, and agents for permission to reprint these works. Adaptations are by Burton Goodman.

"Cemetery Path" by Leonard Q. Ross. Copyright © 1984 by *Saturday Review*. Reprinted by permission of *Saturday Review*.

"Two Thanksgiving Day Gentlemen" by O. Henry. Reprinted by permission of Doubleday, a division of Bantam, Doubleday, Dell Publishing Group, Inc.

"The Dinner Party" by Mona Gardner. Copyright © 1942, 1979 by Mona Gardner. Reprinted by permission of Bill Berger Associates, Inc.

"People of the Third Planet" by Dale Crail. Copyright © 1968 by Scholastic, Inc. Reprinted by permission of Scholastic, Inc.

"The Big Day" by Jack Ritchie. Copyright © 1986 by Western Publishing. Reprinted by permission of Larry Sternig Literary Agency.

"The Open Window" by Saki. From the *Complete Short Stories of Saki* by H. H. Munro. Copyright 1930, renewed © 1958 by The Viking Press, Inc. Reprinted by permission of Viking Penguin Inc.

"Charles." An adaptation of "Charles" from *The Lottery* by Shirley Jackson. Copyright © 1948, 1949 by Shirley Jackson. Copyright renewed © 1976 by Laurence Hyman, Barry Hyman, Mrs. Sarah Webster, and Mrs. Joanne Schnurer. Reprinted by permission of Farrar, Straus & Giroux, Inc. This version appeared in the Scope English Anthology.

"The Getaway" by John Savage. Copyright © 1966 by the Curtis Publishing Company. Reprinted by permission of Curtis Brown, Ltd.

"The Lion Roared" by Virginia Eiseman. Copyright © 1944 by Liberty Magazine, Inc. Reprinted by permission of Liberty Library Corporation.

"The Cage" (originally titled "The Cell") by Martin Raim. Copyright © 1960 by Scholastic, Inc. Reprinted by permission of Scholastic, Inc.

"Two Were Left" by Hugh B. Cave. Copyright © 1942 by the Crowell-Collier Publishing Company. Reprinted by permission of the author.

"The Precious Stones of Axolotyl" by Manuela Williams Crosno. Copyright © 1987 by Manuela Williams Crosno. Reprinted by permission of Manuela Williams Crosno.

"The Immortal Bard" by Isaac Asimov. Copyright © 1953 by Palmer Publication, Inc. Reprinted by permission of Doubleday, a division of Bantam, Doubleday, Dell Publishing Group, Inc.

Progress Chart

1. Write in your score for each exercise.
2. Write in your Total Score.

	T	W	I	S	T	TOTAL SCORE
Story 1						
Story 2						
Story 3						
Story 4						
Story 5						
Story 6						
Story 7						
Story 8						
Story 9						
Story 10						
Story 11						
Story 12						
Story 13						
Story 14						
Story 15						
Story 16						
Story 17						
Story 18						

Progress Graph

1. Write your Total Score in the box under the number for each passage.
2. Put an *x* along the line above each box to show your Total Score for that passage.
3. Make a graph of your progress by drawing a line to connect the *x*'s.

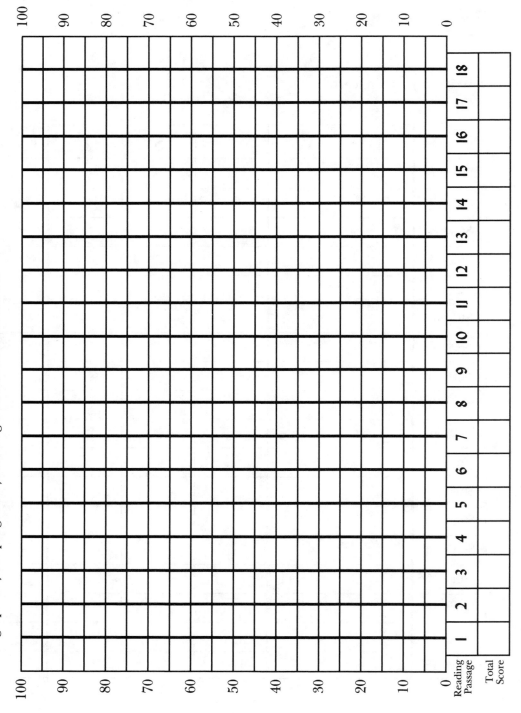

Reading Passage	1	2	3	4	5	6	7	8	9	10	11	12	13	14	15	16	17	18
Total Score																		